Essential Law

Wills, Trusts & Estates

Self-Teaching Guide

3rd edition

STERLING
Education

3   2   1

ISBN-13: 979-8-8855701-5-2

Sterling Education products are available at quantity discounts.

Contact info@sterling–prep.com.

Sterling Education
6 Liberty Square #11
Boston, MA 02109

©2022 Sterling Education
Published by Sterling Education
Printed in the U.S.A.

Customer Satisfaction Guarantee

Your feedback is important because we strive to provide the highest quality prep materials. Email us comments or suggestions.

info@sterling–prep.com

We reply to emails – check your spam folder

STERLING
Education

From the foundations of constitutional law to complex issues of contracts, the *Essential Law Self-Teaching Guide* series is a perfect compendium to help readers understand multifaceted areas of American Law. Created by highly qualified legal professionals with extensive credentials, these books empower readers to expand their understanding of law.

The content is a clearly presented and systematically organized review of legal principles governing various areas of law. It elucidates the concepts of constitutional rights, criminal law, civil procedure, rules of evidence, contracts, torts, real property, family law, estates, wills and trusts, and business associations.

We commend your desire to learn more about the law. The editors sincerely hope that these guides will be a valuable resource for your learning.

Comprehensive Glossary of Legal Terms

Over 2,100 essential legal terms defined and explained. An excellent reference source for law students, practitioners, and readers seeking an understanding of legal vocabulary and its application.

Landmark U.S. Supreme Court Cases: Essential Summaries

Learn important constitutional cases that shaped American law. Understand how the evolving needs of society intersect with the U.S. Constitution. Summaries of seminal Supreme Court cases focused on legal issues, underlying principles, and judicial decisions.

Visit our Amazon store

Everything You Always Wanted to Know About...

Chemistry	American History
Physics	American Law
Cell and Molecular Biology	American Government and Politics
Organismal Biology	Comparative Government and Politics
Psychology	World History
Environmental Science	European History
Human Geography	

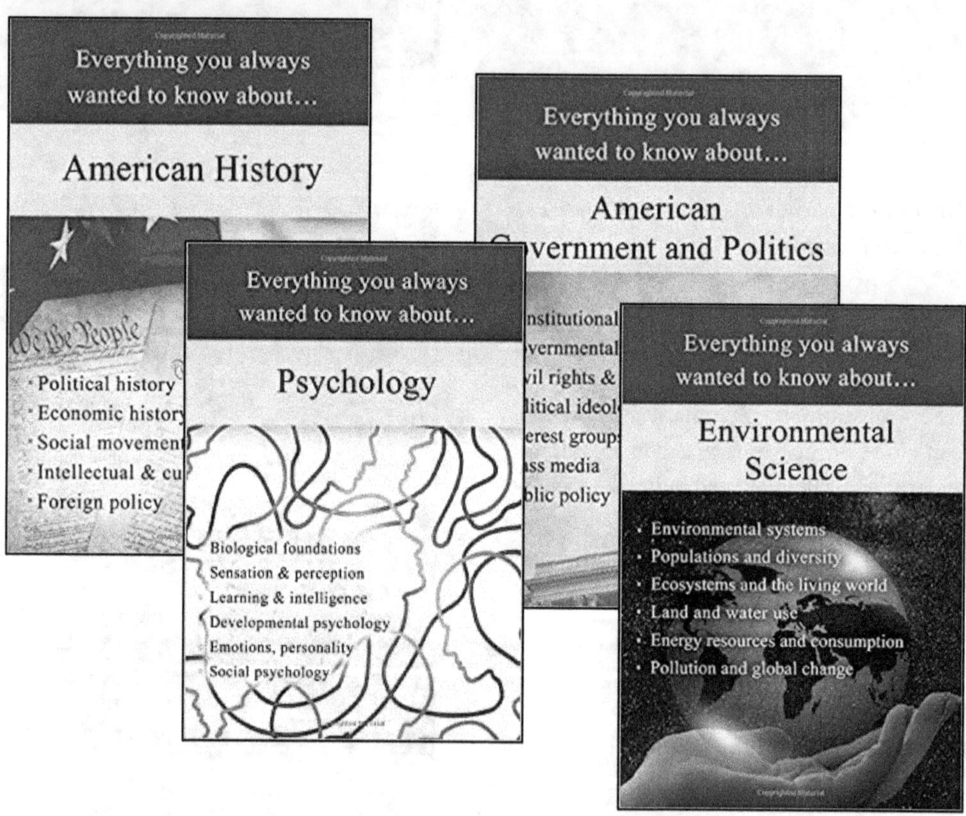

Visit our Amazon store

Table of Contents

GOVERNING LAW (*continued*)

GOVERNING LAW (*continued*)

GOVERNING LAW (*continued*)

GOVERNING LAW (*continued*)

GOVERNING LAW (*continued*)

ANATOMY OF A LAWSUIT (*continued*)

ANATOMY OF A LAWSUIT (*continued*)

APPENDIX (*continued*)

Overview of American Law (*continued*)

U.S. Court Systems – Federal and State Courts ... **161**

How Civil Cases Move Through the Federal Courts ... **169**

APPENDIX (*continued*)

APPENDIX (*continued*)

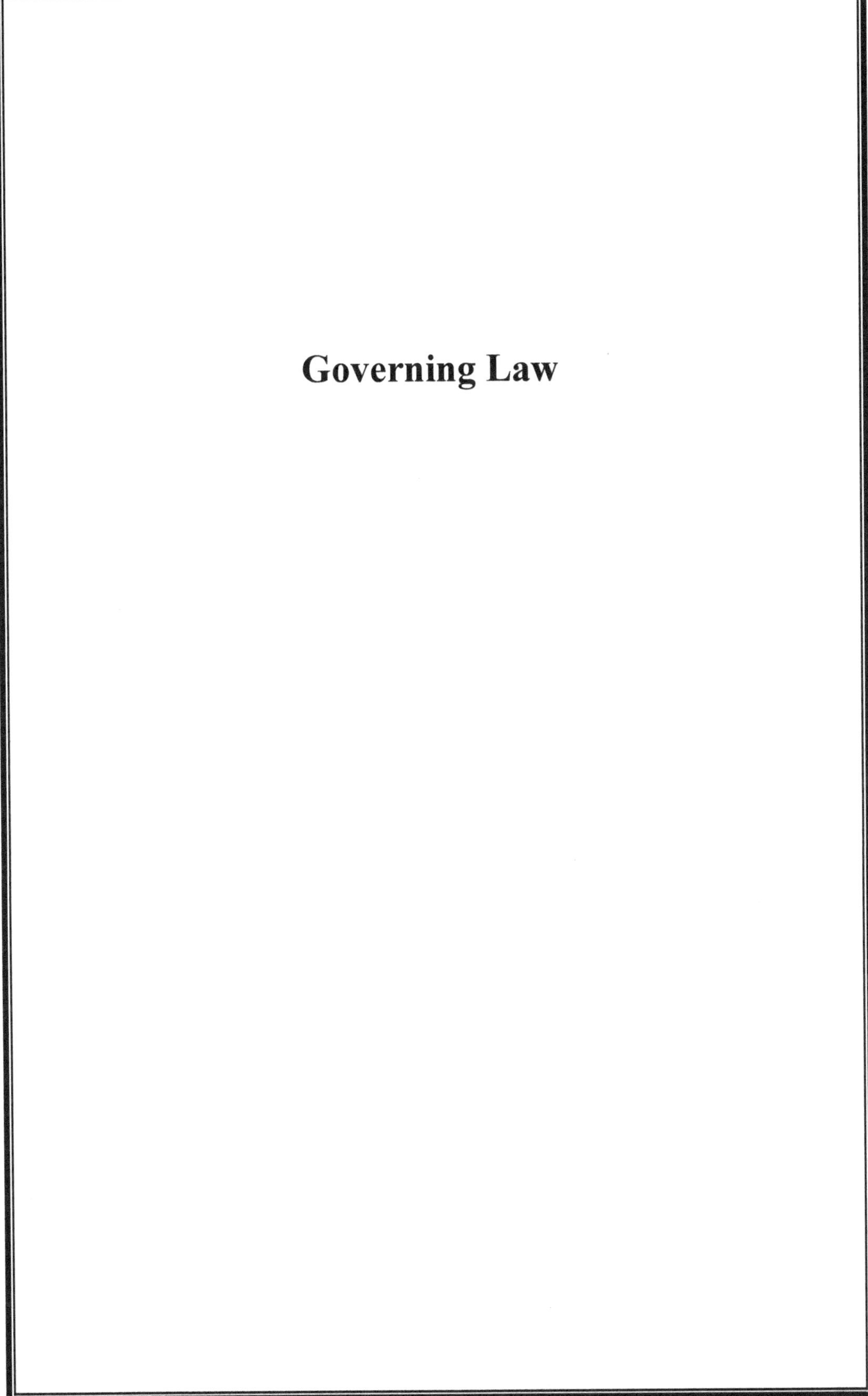

Governing Law

Probate Basics

Disposition of property and possessions

The legal process of transferring property upon a person's death is known as "probate." Although probate customs and laws have changed over time, the purpose has remained much the same: people formalize their intentions as to the transfer of their property at the time of their death (typically in a will), their property is collected, certain debts are paid from the estate, and the remaining property is distributed.

The probate process is a court-supervised process designed to sort out the transfer of a person's property at death. Property subject to probate is owned by a person at death, which does not pass to others by designation or ownership (e.g., life insurance policies and "payable on death" bank accounts).

The expression, *probating a will* describes how a person shows the court that the decedent (person who died) followed legal formalities in drafting their will. There are three primary ways to avoid probate: joint ownership with the right of survivorship (JTROS), gifts, and revocable trusts.

Although the law does not require an executor to be a lawyer or financial expert, it does require that every executor fulfill their duties with the utmost honesty and diligence. This *fiduciary duty* holds the executor to act in good faith regarding a person's will. An executor is *not* entitled to proceeds from the sale of property of the estate. Depending on the state, an executor is entitled to a fee for administering the will. Most states mandate that this fee be reasonable given the size or complexity of the documents and estate.

Role and duties of an executor

An executor is someone named in a will, given the legal responsibility to care for a deceased person's remaining financial obligations. The executor is responsible for locating the deceased's belongings and the individuals named in the will. Typically, individuals tend to choose people whom they trust, so it is undoubtedly an honor. Most executors are immediate family members, with spouses, children, and parents as common executors.

The executor plays a critical role after the testator (the person to whom the will relates) dies, including the tasks of locating assets, paying creditors, and ensuring that beneficiaries named in the will receive property to which they are entitled.

A power of attorney may be necessary while someone is alive, while an executor assumes the role only after death. An executor is responsible for paying the debts and distributing money and property according to the wishes of the deceased.

Executors wind down an estate and perform the following functions:

- Distributing assets according to the will

- Maintaining property until the estate is settled (e.g., upkeep of a house)

- Paying bills for the estate

- Paying taxes on the estate

- Make court appearances for the estate

The executor is generally in charge of making sure the property named in the will goes to the recipient. An executor fulfills many duties depending on the complexity of the will and the property to be distributed. These specific duties typically include:

1) Locate the deceased person's assets and keep them safe until they can be distributed to those named in the will. This includes deciding which assets to sell and which to keep.

2) Decide if probating the last will and testament in court is necessary. Probating a will is the process of getting a court to approve the validity of the will. The decision to probate a will depends on state laws where the will is administered and the property's value passing via the will.

3) Contact people named in a will to inherit money or property.

4) File the will in the appropriate probate court. This is generally required by law, even if the will does not need to go through probate.

5) Finalize the deceased's affairs. This includes canceling credit cards and notifying debtors and creditors about the death. If the deceased person was collecting Social Security benefits, the Social Security Administration should be contacted.

6) Establish a bank account for the estate. Executors are generally required to keep the estate's money separate. Setting up a bank account in the estate's name can make paying off debts to creditors easier.

7) Continue necessary payments. The funds in the estate's bank account can be used to make mortgage, insurance, and other recurring payments that need to be paid during the administration of the will.

8) Pay debts and creditors. In general, before any person named in a will can receive their inheritance, the deceased's debts and creditors need to be paid. The executor should notify creditors and find out how they wish to proceed.

9) Pay final income taxes. Generally, the executor of a will ensures that the deceased's income taxes for the last year they were alive are paid.

10) Distribute property distribution of the deceased's property. Property that is given through a will should be recorded. If the property is not named in the will, it should pass according to the state's intestacy laws.

If a person died without a valid will, their real and personal property is distributed based on intestate succession laws of the state. An administrator facilitates intestacy distribution according to state law.

Probate sequence

The probate process may be contested or uncontested. Most contested issues generally arise in the probate process because a disgruntled heir seeks a larger share of the decedent's property than they received. Arguments often raised include: the decedent may have been improperly influenced in making gifts, the decedent did not know what they were doing (insufficient mental capacity) when the will was executed, and the decedent did not follow the necessary legal formalities in drafting their will. The majority of probated estates, however, are uncontested.

The basic process of probating an estate includes:

- Collecting all probate property of the decedent

- Paying all debts, claims, and taxes owed by the estate

- Collecting all rights to income, dividends, etc.

- Settling any disputes, and

- Distributing the remaining property to the heirs

Usually, the decedent names a person (executor) to manage his or her affairs upon death. If the decedent fails to name an executor, the court will appoint a personal representative, or administrator, to settle the estate. The administrator will fulfill many of the same duties as an executor.

Typically, people may leave property to any person they wish and make such designations in their will. However, in certain situations, depending on the relationship to the decedent and the laws of the state, the decedent's wishes may have to be overridden by the court. For example, in most states, a spouse is entitled to a certain amount of property. Furthermore, creditors may have a claim on the property of the estate.

Each jurisdiction prescribes how long an estate must be open to give creditors adequate time to present claims to the estate. The more complex and sizable the estate, the longer and more time-consuming this process can be.

Intestacy: dying without a will or trust

Dying without a will means dying *intestate*. The intestacy laws of the state where the decedent resided determine how property is distributed upon their death. This includes any bank accounts, securities, real estate, and other assets owned at the time of death. Real estate owned in a different state than the decedent's resident state will be settled under the state's intestacy laws where the property is located.

According to state law, when a person dies without a valid will, their property passes by intestate succession to heirs. All states have laws (or *statutes*) for intestacy and escheat.

The laws of intestate succession depend on marital status and children. In most cases, the property is distributed in split shares to "heirs," which could include a surviving spouse, parents, siblings, aunts and uncles, nieces, nephews, and distant relatives. Generally, when no relatives can be found, the estate escheats to the state.

The purpose of intestate succession statutes is to distribute the decedent's wealth in a manner that closely represents how the average person would have designed their estate plan had that person had a will. This default distribution can differ dramatically from what the person would have wanted. Even where it is known what the person intended, no exceptions are made without a valid will. There are no exceptions based on need or special circumstances.

Single and without a will

A single person without children has parents who receive the entire estate if they are both living. Otherwise, it will be divided among siblings (including half-siblings) and surviving parents if one parent has already died. Without surviving parents at the time of death, the estate is divided among siblings in equal parts. If there are no surviving parents, siblings, or descendants of siblings (nieces and nephews), then the relatives on the mother's side inherit one-half of the estate, with the other one-half passing to the relatives on the father's side.

A single person without children has the entire estate pas to the children, in equal shares. If any child has died before the decedent and has children, then that child's share goes to the grandchildren.

Married and without a will

Depending on how assets are owned at the time of death, the estate will either go entirely to a surviving spouse (community or marital property) or split between a surviving spouse, siblings, and parents (if it is separate property). If the decedent is married and has children with the current spouse, the entire estate passes to the surviving spouse. Otherwise, the surviving spouse receives up to one-half of the estate, with the remaining portion passing to the surviving children from another spouse or partner.

Unmarried Couples without a will

Dying without a will can be devastating to unmarried couples living together. Because intestacy laws only recognize relatives, unmarried couples do not inherit the property of their partner who dies without a will. Unless there is a will that clearly states a person's intentions when they die, the decedent's property will be divided among relatives, depending on their relation to the decedent.

State laws on intestate succession

States have laws on estates and probate determining who inherits property when someone dies without a will. When a person dies without a valid will, their estate passes to heirs or family members classes by intestate succession, as prescribed by state law. There are certain legal terms and specific rules on intestate succession. The purpose of intestate succession statutes is to distribute the decedent's property in an organized and methodical way. States have enacted laws that determine how the property will be distributed.

Property distributed by intestate succession

Generally, heirs are grouped in classes created to determine the order of whom the property will transfer to and the share of property among individual heirs. The share of the property depends on who survives the decedent. For example, in most states, if a person dies with no surviving spouse but with three children, the children will take the entire estate. However, if the person dies with a surviving spouse and three children, the surviving spouse may take half of the entire estate and the other half to three children.

The classes of heirs include the following:

- The decedent's surviving spouse

- Descendants (children, grandchildren, and so on)

- Parents

- Descendants of decedent's parents (siblings, nieces, and nephews)

- Descendants of grandparents (aunts and uncles)

If none of the individuals above exist, the property may escheat to the state.

Debts of a deceased relative

After a relative dies, the last thing grieving family members may expect is calls from debt collectors asking them to pay their deceased loved one's outstanding debts. According to the Federal Trade Commission (FTC), a surviving relative usually has no legal obligation to pay the debts of a family member who has died. The Fair Debt Collection Practices Act (FDCPA) protects the rights of surviving relatives, which prohibits debt collectors from using abusive, unfair, or deceptive practices to collect debts.

Under the FDCPA, which the FTC enforces, a debt collector regularly collects debts owed to others. This includes collection agencies, lawyers who collect debts regularly, parties buying delinquent debts, and collecting.

Generally, an estate is responsible for paying debts. However, if there is not enough in the estate to cover the debts, they typically go unpaid. There is no legal obligation to pay the debts of a deceased relative who was not a spouse. Even a spouse's obligation to pay may be limited under state probate law.

The Uniform Probate Code

The Uniform Probate Code (the Code) serves as the basis of many state laws. Nevertheless, the laws of states can vary greatly and from the Code itself. Under the Code, close relatives take property instead of distant relatives. The classes of relatives whose members receive property under the Code include the decedent's surviving spouse, descendants (i.e., children, grandchildren, etc.), parents, descendants of decedent's parents (i.e., siblings, nieces, nephews), grandparents, and descendants of grandparents (i.e., aunts, uncles, cousins). Adopted descendants are treated the same as biological descendants.

If none of those named classes of relatives include persons qualified to take the estate, the property "escheats" (i.e., goes by default) to the state.

Surviving spouse share

Under the Code, a surviving spouse is entitled to the entire estate (after expenses and taxes of the decedent) or a substantial part. The surviving spouse is entitled to the entire net estate if the decedent is also survived by the children of the decedent and the surviving spouse.

The surviving spouse is entitled to the entire net estate if descendants and parents do not survive the decedent.

If parents survive, but no descendants survive, a surviving spouse takes the first statutory amount (e.g., $200,000) of the net estate plus an amount (e.g., three-fourths) of any excess.

If the decedent is survived by descendants who are also the descendants of the surviving spouse and by descendants who are not descendants of the surviving spouse, the surviving spouse takes the first $150,000 of the net estate plus one-half of anything exceeding that amount.

If the decedent is not survived by any descendants who are also descendants of the surviving spouse but is survived by descendants who are not descendants of the surviving spouse, the surviving spouse takes the first $100,000 of the net estate plus one-half of anything exceeding that amount.

Descendants share

Under the Code, if no spouse survives but descendants of the decedent survive, the descendants take the entire net estate by "right of representation."

Under the Code, if a spouse or descendants do not survive a decedent, the entire net estate passes to the decedent's parents equally or, if only one survives, to the survivor.

Under the Code, if a decedent is not survived by a spouse, descendants, or parents, the entire net estate passes to the decedent's parent's descendants (siblings of the decedent). If there are no siblings or descendants of siblings, the net estate goes to the decedent's grandparents or descendants.

Notes for active learning

The Probate Estate

Distribution of the estate

The law of wills, the rules of intestate distribution, and the laws governing estates' administration apply to the assets which are in the probate estate of the decedent.

The assets in the probate estate are held in the name of the decedent at the time of death.

The following property is not held solely in the decedent's name is not in the probate estate.

Partnership property

Partnership property, absent a specific provision in the partnership agreement, vests in the remaining partners at death.

The asset, which is in the estate of the deceased partner, is the right to an accounting of the value of the deceased's partnership assets.

Many partnership agreements modify this rule and permit the estate to remain as a partner or provide a mechanism whereby the deceased partner's interest is liquidated.

Property held in a fiduciary capacity

Property held by the decedent as a trustee (i.e., fiduciary) does not vest in the executor but must be turned over to the successor fiduciary.

Jointly-held property

Real and personal property held between the decedent and another as joint tenants or property held between the decedent and their spouse as tenants by the entirety passes directly to the surviving joint tenant. It is not part of the probate estate.

Completed gifts

An irrevocable gift made by the decedent during their lifetime, either outright or in trust, is vested in the donee or the trustee and is not part of the probate estate.

Causes of action – survival

Lawsuits pending and which survive death are assets of the probate estate.

Suits that survive death in which the decedent was a defendant can be prosecuted against the estate.

Contract actions and tort actions for personal injury survive death.

Intangible tort actions, such as libel, slander, and deceit, do not survive death. The estate cannot recover on such actions, nor is it liable for such actions brought because of actions of the decedent.

Causes of action – wrongful death actions

Actions to recover for the conscious pain and suffering and lost wages which the decedent suffered while living are assets of the probate estate.

Proceeds received from actions for wrongful death, while brought by the executor in the name of the decedent death actions, are not assets of the probate estate. These proceeds are distributed primarily to the surviving spouse and children per a statutory formula.

Life insurance and rights under pension plans

Insurance on the life of the decedent, even if the decedent was the owner of the life insurance policy, which is payable to a named beneficiary, is paid directly to the named beneficiary and is not an asset of the probate estate.

The decedent's pension plan proceeds, naming an individual as a beneficiary after the death of the decedent pass outside the probate estate.

Intestate Distribution of Estate

Complete and partial intestacy

Most exams have a question that requires applying the laws of descent and distribution.

The most common way for applying the law of intestacy is when an actor in a question dies without a will, and the examinee must determine how their estate should be distributed.

A complete or partial intestacy occurs when a will does not entirely dispose of the decedent's assets. This occurs if the will has no residuary clause or does not effectively dispose of the probate estate assets.

Even if an heir has been disinherited in the body of the will, they take by intestacy if the will fails to dispose of all assets.

The estate will be distributed by the intestacy law, where a will is declared invalid, and there is no prior will that governs the estate's distribution.

If a trust does not entirely dispose of its assets, which would occur when the final distribution is to the children or issue of a named beneficiary and that beneficiary does not have children or issue, the assets are disposed of by intestate distribution.

Intestate distribution laws are applied as if the settlor had died at the time when there was a failure of distribution, not at the time of the settlor's death.

Statutory disposition

The laws of intestate distribution apply to the net probate estate, which are assets remaining in the probate estate after the payment of debts, expenses of administration, funeral expenses, and taxes.

Spouse survives

Determining if a spouse survived the decedent presents two issues:

1) the person who claims the position of a surviving spouse must be validly married to the decedent and not divorced from the decedent when the decedent died, and

2) the person who was the spouse must survive the decedent. If their deaths were simultaneous, the simultaneous death act discussed below applies.

Spouse and issue survive

Issue includes the decedent's descendants whether, by blood or adoption, and includes children, grandchildren, great-grandchildren, etc.

If a surviving spouse and the decedent are survived by issue, that surviving spouse takes one-half of the net probate estate by intestacy.

The issue takes the other half per the rules for the distribution of the estate among the issue.

Spouse and kindred survive

If the decedent has a surviving spouse but no surviving descendants but is survived by kindreds (i.e., related persons to the decedent) such as parents, siblings, nieces, nephews, aunts, uncles, or cousins, the surviving spouse takes a statutory amount (e.g., the first $300,000) of the net probate estate and one-half of the remaining probate estate.

The kindred take half above the statutory amount.

For example, the decedent has a surviving spouse and a surviving mother and father, and the estate is $600,000. The surviving spouse takes $450,000 (statutory amount plus ½ in excess), and the mother and father take $75,000 each.

Spouse survives, but no issue or kindred survive

If a spouse survives without issue or kindred, the surviving spouse takes the entire probate estate.

Issue survive

If the decedent is survived by issue and there is no surviving spouse or the surviving spouse does not take their portion, the entire net probate estate is allocated to issue.

If children survive the decedent, that property reserved for issue passes in equal shares to the surviving children and to issue of any deceased child by right of representation.

If no children are surviving, the property is divided equally among grandchildren with a right of representation for the children of a deceased grandchild who is survived by issue.

No issue survive, but parents survive

If the decedent is not survived by issue, property not allocated to a surviving spouse is divided equally to the surviving parents.

No issue and no parents survive, but siblings or their issue survive

If there is no surviving issue or parents, property not allocated to a surviving spouse passes to the decedent's siblings, including half-siblings (i.e., persons with one parent in common with the decedent).

Issue of a deceased sibling, nephews, nieces, and their issue, take their deceased parent's share by right of representation as long as one sibling survives.

If there are no surviving siblings, property not allocated to a surviving spouse is inherited by nephews and nieces in equal shares with the issue of a deceased nephew or niece taking their parent's share by right of representation.

If those taking are in the same generation, they share equally; otherwise, they take equally in the older generation with children of deceased members of that generation taking their parent's share by right of representation.

No issue, parents, siblings, or their issue survive

If neither issue, parents, siblings, nor their issue survives, property not allocated to a surviving spouse passes in equal shares to the next of kin of the same degree of kindred.

The degree of kinship is determined by counting from the decedent up to the decedent's common ancestors and the next of kin and counting down to the next of kin.

For example, a first cousin is of the fourth degree of kindred because two degrees are used by counting to the common grandparent and two degrees counting down to the level of a cousin.

For example, a first cousin once removed is of the fifth degree of kindred.

For collateral kin of equal degree claim through different ancestors, those claiming the nearest ancestor are preferred.

Escheat

If a spouse and nor kindred survive, the property escheats to the state.

Additional rules of intestate distribution

A person adopted is a child of their adoptive parents for purposes of intestate distribution.

They take as an heir from their adoptive parents and the position of a child of their adoptive parents in determining their right to inherit from their adoptive parent's relatives.

An adopted child loses their status as a child of their natural parents when determining their right to inherit from them or their kindred.

The exception is that a child adopted by a spouse of a natural parent after the other natural parent dies retains the right to inherit from the relatives of the deceased natural parent.

When an adopted child dies intestate and is not survived by issue, their heirs are determined as if they had been born to their adoptive parents.

Half-blood

Children with one common parent are siblings for intestacy purposes and inherit an equal share with persons who have two common parents.

Children born out of wedlock

A child born out of wedlock is always a child of their mother for purposes of intestate succession, even if deemed an illegitimate child.

A child born out of wedlock is deemed a legitimate child of both parents for intestacy purposes if their parents have intermarried and the father has acknowledged them as his child or been adjudged as the father.

A child born out of wedlock who is illegitimate may inherit from and through their father:

> 1) if the father acknowledged paternity, or

> 2) if, during their lifetime or after death, the decedent has been adjudged in a judicial proceeding to be the father.

An illegitimate child may initiate a judicial proceeding to establish paternity after the decedent's death.

The descendants of a deceased illegitimate child may take their share by representation if paternity of the illegitimate has been acknowledged or established if paternity has not been acknowledged or judicially established, an illegitimate child cannot take as a child under intestacy laws.

If an illegitimate person dies intestate without issue, their mother or relatives are their heirs.

For their father and relatives to take by intestacy, the father–child relationship must be established by the father's acknowledgment of the child or through judicial proceedings.

Posthumous children

A child born to a married woman after her husband's death is a child of the deceased husband under intestacy laws.

The fatherhood of a child born out of wedlock after the father's death can be judicially established.

Limitation of rights of heir or legatee who kills testator

Some states have no statute which limits the rights of heir or legatees who kill the testator to inherit from their estate but imposes a constructive trust on the assets which such a person would receive and redistributes them to those who would inherit if the murderer predeceased the testator.

Notes for active learning

Execution of Wills

A will is a declaration of how a person wants their property to be distributed upon their death. It is a testamentary distribution of property. The person who makes the will is the testator or testatrix (if female). Every state has a Statute of Wills that establishes the requirements for making a valid will in that state.

Contract to make a will

A contract to make a will containing specific provisions is valid if it is in writing.

The consideration for such a contract is often that the other party will make a reciprocal will.

If the testator violates their contractual obligation by executing a will that does not contain the provisions obligated by contract, the will executed is valid, but the person holding the contractual obligation can impress the estate with a constructive trust to dispose of the assets following the contractual obligation.

A critical issue in many questions is the devolution of the property after death and assesses whether an instrument described in the question is a valid will.

To intelligently discuss that issue, apply the following law.

Age for capacity to execute a will

A person must be eighteen years of age or older to execute a valid will.

Testamentary capacity

The testator must be of sound mind; that is, must understand in a general way:

1) the nature and extent of their property

2) the natural objects of their bounty; and

3) the nature of their act of making a will.

In a contest over the validity of a will, the will's proponent, usually the named executor, has the burden of proving that the testator was of sound mind when the will was executed.

The testator is presumed to be of sound mind until the opponents of the validity of the will introduce credible evidence that the testator lacked testamentary capacity.

The proponent of the will has the burden of persuasion on the issue and must prove capacity by a preponderance of the evidence.

In such a will contest, three classes of persons are competent to give an opinion on the soundness of the testator's mind when the will was executed:

1) witnesses to the will;

2) the testator's physician; and

3) a psychiatrist or other person who can qualify as an expert on sanity.

Other persons may testify in a will contest concerning facts upon which conclusions about the testator's sound mind can be based.

Testamentary intent

For a document to be a valid will, the testator must sign it with the understanding of making a will.

A document is ineffective as a will if the testator intends that it is a joke or solely designed to accomplish some purpose other than disposing of their property at death.

If the testator executes a will conditioned on some event occurring and it does not occur, the will is revoked.

The testator must generally know and approve the contents but need not know the technical details contained in it.

Written requirements for the execution of a valid will

A will must be entirely in writing.

A nuncupative will (an oral disposition of personal property) may be used only by a soldier in actual military service or a mariner at sea.

Oral wills are otherwise invalid.

Signature required by the testator or at their express direction

The writing must be signed by the testator or another in their presence and express direction.

If the testator intends the writing to be their signature executing the document, which they assert as their will, the testator may sign or make a mark on any part of the will.

Proper attestation

Holographic wills are entirely in the testator's handwriting and not valid unless attested or executed in a jurisdiction that recognizes the validity of unattested holographic wills.

The testator's signature must be properly attested to by two witnesses.

The testator need not sign the instrument in the presence of the witnesses.

If the testator does not sign in their presence, the testator must show their signature to each attesting witness, acknowledge that the signature is theirs, and ask them to sign the will as attesting witnesses in the testator's presence.

The will is valid even if a witness did not see the testator's signature if the witness could have seen it if they had wished.

The witnesses must know that they are witnessing a will but need not read it or be aware of its contents.

A competent witness can be any person of enough understanding when a subscribing witness, even if a minor.

A person who affixes the testator's signature to the will at their express direction may serve as a witness to the will.

A will is valid even if the witness is dead or incompetent when offered for probate.

The witness's signature can be proven by persons who saw them sign the will or identify the witness's signature.

At a probate proceeding where the validity of the will is in issue, the witness need not have a present memory of executing the will if they identify their signature as a subscribing witness.

The witnesses do not have to reside in the jurisdiction where the testator is domiciled.

Interested witnesses

Most jurisdictions stipulate that interested parties, such as a beneficiary or the attorney who drafted the will, cannot be witnesses. If an interested party has attested to a will, state law either voids any clauses that benefit such person or voids the entire will.

A person who signs the will as one of the two necessary attesting witnesses and receives a legacy or devise under the will is an interested witness.

The fact that the witness was interested does not invalidate the will.

The legacy or devise to an interested witness or an interested witness's spouse is void.

If there are more than two witnesses to the will, the interested witness's signature is superfluous, and the legacy to that witness is valid.

If the witness is not named a legatee or devisee in the will but takes because of an anti-lapse statute's operation, their legacy is valid.

A witness is not considered an interested witness because they are named executor but receives no legacy of a will.

He does not forfeit their appointment as executor because they witnessed the will.

The signature of a person as a witness to a will who is an officer or director of a charity named a beneficiary of the will does not void that charity's legacy.

If a legacy is void because the legatee was a necessary witness to the will, that legacy is treated like a lapsed legacy. An alternative legatee takes, or if there is no alternative legatee, the residue is increased by the void legacy.

If the void legacy is the sole residuary legacy, or there is no residue clause in the will, the amount of the void disposition is distributed per the laws of intestacy.

If there is more than one residuary legatee, and the legacy to one of them is void because that residuary legatee was an interested witness, the residuary legatee is divided among the other residuary legatees proportionately unless the will indicates a contrary intent.

Codicils

Once a will has been validly executed, it cannot be altered or amended except by an instrument executed following the requirements for a valid will.

If the testator changes the content of the will on the face of the will by adding a new legatee or substituting one legatee for another, the changes are invalid, and the will, as initially executed, will be considered the testator's will.

An exception to this rule is the doctrine of partial revocation.

If the testator only crosses out a specific part of the will, that act is considered a partial revocation of that portion.

A will can be changed by a codicil (i.e., a document that alters an existing will) executed with the same formalities as a will.

A codicil modifies rather than replaces the will's provisions unless a contrary intent is clear.

A validly executed codicil republishes the will on the codicil's date.

A challenge to the original will cannot be sustained unless the challenge is also effective against the codicil.

A properly drafted codicil should explicitly refer to the will.

Revocation and Revival of Wills

Will revocation

Even if it is concluded that a will is valid, determine that it has not been revoked before using its provisions to dispose of the decedent's estate.

Events in the testator's life such as marriage and divorce occurring after the will is executed and before death revokes a will either wholly or partially.

The voluntary action of the testator may revoke a will in two ways.

Revocation by an instrument executed in the same manner

The testator can revoke a will by another instrument executed and attested to in the same manner as a will.

The instrument that frequently revokes a will is a subsequent will that typically contains language explicitly revoking prior wills and codicils.

The subsequent instrument may contain no dispositive language and only contain language revoking prior wills, in which case the intestacy laws would govern the estate's devolution.

If an instrument revokes part of a will, it is considered a codicil.

If the subsequent will is not valid, it does not revoke the earlier will.

Revocation by intentional destruction

The testator may revoke a will wholly or partially by performing a physical act on the will itself to revoke it in whole or in part.

Crossing out specific paragraphs of a will is a partial revocation of those sections.

If the testator, with intent to revoke a will, causes physical destruction of the paper by tearing or burning it, the entire will is revoked.

Defacing the will by writing canceled over the writing in the document revokes it.

An unwitnessed notation signed by the testator declaring the will revoked is not enough.

There is a presumption that a will that cannot be found was revoked.

That presumption can be rebutted by producing secondary evidence of its contents and showing that the testator did not intend its destruction.

The scrivener can testify to the contents of the will because the attorney-client privilege is inapplicable in probate proceedings dealing with a will's validity.

Intentional destruction of one of two duplicate wills constitutes a revocation.

Conditional or dependent relative revocation

If the revocation of a will occurred by a physical act conditioned upon the valid execution of a new will, the new will is not valid because it was improperly executed. The revocation is not valid, and the old will continues to be operative.

Revival of revoked wills

A will that has been revoked by a subsequent will is not automatically revived if the subsequent will is thereafter revoked.

If the testator's intent at the time they revoked the subsequent will is to reinstate a prior will, the court will revive the prior will.

Special Circumstances Affecting Intestate and Testate Distribution

Simultaneous death

The Uniform Simultaneous Death Act applies if the order of death of two or more individuals cannot be determined by affirmative proof.

If there is valid forensic evidence or eyewitness testimony that one person lived longer than the other, this Act does not apply.

The Act applies to the interpretation of the effect of wills and the application of intestacy laws.

Its Act's provisions are frequently tested in Wills' questions.

The mechanics of its operation should be committed to memory.

The basic principle of the Act is that in determining a person's estate whose death coincided, conclusively presume that the decedent survived the other person whose death coincided.

Thus, inconsistent facts are applied to the estate of each decedent.

The specific rules are:

1) A legatee or devisee in a will or a person entitled to take under the intestacy laws who died simultaneously is deemed to have predeceased the decedent whose estate is being distributed. Therefore, the rules of lapsed legacies apply.

2) If the two persons who died simultaneously held property as joint tenants or as tenants by the entirety, then for one half of the property, one joint tenant is deemed to have survived, and the second joint tenant is deemed to have survived for the other half.

Half of the jointly held property is considered an asset of the estate of each who died simultaneously. That estate is probated as if the holder of the other half of the joint tenancy has predeceased them.

3) The named beneficiary in an insurance policy predeceased the insured.

The insurance policy proceeds would thus be payable to the alternative beneficiary or the deceased's estate if there is no alternative beneficiary.

For a question involving simultaneous deaths, determine which assets, including jointly held assets, are in the estate of each decedent and determine how the estate is to be distributed as if the other person who died simultaneously had predeceased the decedent.

Advancement

Property which the decedent gives during their lifetime to an heir, with the intent that the gift satisfies wholly or partially the share to which the donee would be entitled from the donor's estate is an advancement.

The amount of the *inter-vivos* gift is added to the intestate estate. The larger amount is divided by the number of shares in the estate to determine each beneficiary's amount.

The amount of the advancement is deducted from the share of the heir who received it.

An *inter-vivos* gift is an advancement only if the donor describes the gift as an advancement in writing or if the donee acknowledges the gift as an advancement in writing.

The advancement is its fair market value at the date of the gift or the amount in which the donor states the value to be at the date of the gift.

Renunciation of property interests

A person may disclaim in whole or in part any interest passing to them as the result of the decedent's death by filing a signed disclaimer in probate court (and in the registry of deeds where disclaimed realty is located) within the statutory time (e.g., nine months) after the donee became entitled to the property.

Once filed, a disclaimer is irrevocable and becomes the property of the person who would have taken it if the disclaiming party had died immediately before the event, which entitled the disclaiming party to receive the property.

Limitations on testamentary dispositions

The decedent's right to make an effective testamentary disposition is limited by considerations of public policy set forth in statutes.

Spouse's elective share

In wills questions requiring to determine which individuals take which parts of the estate, always consider the rights of a surviving spouse to take an elective share and compare the size of that share to the amount which the surviving spouse would take under the will.

Property that the spouse receives as a surviving joint owner or from the proceeds of an insurance policy or through *inter-vivos* gifts does not count against their elective share.

A surviving spouse has a statutory right to waive the provisions of the will and claim the statutory elective share.

This right must be exercised by a writing filed in the Registry of Probate within the statutory time (e.g., six months) after the decedent's will has been allowed.

The spouse's elective share (calculated on the net probate estate) is computed by one of three formulae depending on the other heirs.

To file for an elective share, the person claiming to be the surviving spouse must be validly married to the person claiming to be the surviving spouse at the time of their death and not be a party against whom a separate support action has been filed.

If issue survive

If the decedent is survived by issue, the spouse takes one-third of the net probate estate.

If the amount of the net probate estate is more than $75,000 so that the elective share would exceed $25,000, the spouse receives only $25,000 outright and a life interest in the amount by which the one-third share exceeds $25,000.

The spouse receives a life estate in the portion of the estate, which is real property, and a life interest in a trust fund for the remaining amount in which they are entitled as a life interest.

If kin survive, but no issue survive

If the decedent is survived by kin but no issue, the spouse takes the first $25,000 of the net probate estate outright, plus the income from one-half of the remaining probate estate.

If no issue or kin survive

If the decedent is not survived by issue or kin, the spouse takes $25,000 outright plus one-half of the remaining probate estate outright.

If a spouse has deserted the decedent spouse, or in a case where the decedent spouse was living apart from the surviving spouse under a probate decree of separate support for a justifiable cause, the spouse has no right to waive the will.

The right to waive the will and take a statutory forced share is personal to the spouse and terminates if they die before waiving the will.

The will may not be waived by the executor of the surviving spouse's estate.

Acceptance of any benefits under the will bar the right to waive.

Property held in a revocable *inter vivos* trust where the decedent was settlor, sole trustee, and life income beneficiary is part of the probate estate for purposes of computing the amount of the estate to which the election statute applies.

Some states do not have a statute that calculates the amount to which the waiver statute applies by including jointly held property, completed *inter-vivos* gifts, proceeds of life insurance, and the value of property held in trust for the benefit of the deceased spouse.

When making the waiver-of-the-will calculation, not all states deduct the amounts contained in the above categories, which are now the property of the surviving spouse.

Children not mentioned in the will (pretermitted children)

In will fact patterns where the decedent is survived by a child or by the children of a deceased child, who is not mentioned in the will, consider the possibility that the child is pretermitted (i.e., not mentioned in the will) and has the right to claim their intestate share.

A child can be pretermitted whether born before or after the date when the will was executed.

There are three ways in which a testator can prevent a child or grandchild of a deceased child from being pretermitted.

1) He can leave the child or grandchild a legacy of any size.

2) The testator can indicate that the omission was intentional and not caused by mistake. The easiest way to show intent is to state that intent in the will.

3) He can make provisions for that child during their lifetime.

The terms "accident" or "mistake" do not refer to facts that led the testator to omit the child intentionally but instead to error or mistake in drafting and executing the will.

For example, if the testator says that they make no provision for Son because Son stole from them, Son is not a pretermitted child even if the testator was mistaken about the theft.

The executor and the persons who oppose the child's claim have the burden of showing that the omission was not caused by accident or mistake.

The pretermitted child must file a claim against the estate for their intestate share.

No pretermitted child can take a share in real property unless a claim is filed in the Registry of Probate within one year after approval of the executor's bond.

The intestate share paid to the pretermitted child is first paid out of the estate's residue and from devisees and legatees proportionally.

An illegitimate child cannot be a pretermitted child.

No limitations on charitable bequests

Some states have no statutory provisions limiting the proportion of an estate that may be left to charity nor limiting charitable bequests made in a will executed close to death.

Provisions in restraint of marriage

The testator cannot validly require that a legacy be forfeited if the beneficiary marries.

The testator can condition a testamentary disposition upon a legatee not marrying a person outside of their religion.

Courts are likely to construe a provision that appears to be an absolute restraint on marriage as a provision for a beneficiary's support while that beneficiary is single.

Such a provision in a trust which supports a beneficiary until that beneficiary is married would be upheld.

Notes for active learning

Interpretation and Construction of Wills

Incorporation by reference

A will may incorporate a document, even ones not executed with the formalities of a will if it:

1) was in existence when the will was executed and

2) is identified by clear and satisfactory proof as the paper referred to in the will.

The doctrine has been expanded by statute for revocable *inter vivos* trusts.

The dispositive provisions of an existing revocable *inter vivos* trust may be incorporated by reference into a will even though the trust is revocable or amendable.

If the trust is amended after the will is executed, the document incorporated into the will is the trust as amended.

The devise or bequest to the trustee of a revocable *inter vivos* trust lapses if the trust is revoked or terminated before the testator's death.

Facts of independent significance

A will may provide for the designation of a beneficiary or the amount of a disposition by reference to some future unattested act occurring after the execution of the will if the future act has some significance apart from the will.

For example, a bequest of "one week's wages to those persons in my employ at the date of my death" has two facts that control the recipients' identity and the amount they are to receive, which will be determined after the will has been executed.

Each of these two facts has significance outside of the will itself.

Alterations and interlineations

A new provision inserted after a will was duly executed is invalid, but the will remains valid.

For alterations to the text of the will, they are valid if made before the will was signed.

The proponents of the will have the burden of proving that the alterations were made before the will was signed.

If the testator has struck out a provision of the will after the will was signed, that provision is revoked because a will may be wholly or partially revoked by defacing the instrument itself.

Ambiguities

Extrinsic evidence to explain or contradict the terms of a will is inadmissible unless the will is ambiguous, even if the language of the will was contrary to the intent which the testator expressed orally.

Patent ambiguities

Patent ambiguities appear on the face of the will. For example, the same parcel of property is devised for two different beneficiaries in two separate paragraphs of the will. Extrinsic evidence is not admissible to resolve such ambiguity. The instrument is construed from its language alone or according to general rules of construction.

A mistake may cause the patent ambiguity in the *factum*, a mistake in the will itself, such as an inaccurate description of the property or an erroneous identification of legatee.

Usually, a will may not be corrected for a mistake in the *factum*.

The testator refers to a person (e.g., "my wife"), but the language does not accurately describe their legal relationship; the court will ignore the erroneous legal description.

Latent ambiguities

Latent ambiguities occur when there is no inconsistency in the language of the will itself, but extrinsic facts give rise to ambiguity.

For example, the will may devise $20,000 to Aunt Angela. The testator had two aunts named Angela because their mother and father each had a sister named Angela.

Where there is such a latent ambiguity, extrinsic evidence is admissible to aid in interpreting the will.

Construction of Terms for Relationship and Survivorship

Heirs and next of kin

The terms *heirs* and *next of kin* ordinarily mean persons who inherit by intestacy at the time of the decedent's death.

If the time for the interest of heirs or next of kin to vest is later, the terms include persons who would have been the decedent's heirs at that later date.

For example, if the testator devises a life estate "to my wife for life and then to my heirs," the heirs are those who would have taken if the testator had died at the time that the life estate in the testator's wife terminated.

Then living

The term *then living* requires that the person taking the remainder interest be alive when the prior estate terminates.

Adopted children

Unless a contrary intent plainly appears by the instrument's terms, adopted children are treated the same as natural children in construing the words "child," "grandchild," "issue," "heir," or "heir-at-law."

Construction of devises

If a will devises real estate and does not specify the quality of the estate conveyed, the devise is in fee simple or, if the testator cannot devise a fee simple, the greatest estate the testator could devise.

Exercise of a general power of appointment

The residuary clause of a will does not exercise a general power of appointment held by the testator unless it shows an intent to exercise that power.

If the general power of appointment is not exercised, the assets of the trust in which the power of appointment was held will go by way of the provisions of the trust controlling a default in the exercise of the power of appointment.

If there is no default provision, the property in the trust would go to the heirs of the settlor determined as of the time of the failure to exercise the power of appointment.

Notes for active learning

Changes in Property, Beneficiaries and Marital Status Before Death

While the will is executed during the testator's life, it does not become operative until death.

During that time, changes can occur in the testator's marital status, the testator's property, and the individuals who are beneficiaries of the will.

Each of these changes affects how the will disposes of property at the death of the decedent.

Classification of testamentary dispositions

Testamentary dispositions are classified per the assets of the estate available to pay them.

A specific devise or bequest disposes of an identified item of property owned by the testator and, except in extraordinary circumstances, can only be paid by delivering that asset.

A demonstrative bequest is a gift payable primarily from a specified source and, if that source is inadequate, the estate's general assets can be used to pay it.

A general or pecuniary bequest is payable from the estate's general assets rather than requiring distribution from specific assets.

A residuary disposition is a gift of whatever remains in the estate after claims and other dispositions have been satisfied.

Effect of change in assets between execution and death

The property, which is the subject of a specific bequest, is adeemed, and the beneficiary receives nothing if the testator does not own that asset at the time of death.

Specific bequests – ademption by extinction

An item purchased to replace the asset is not the subject of the specific bequest.

For real estate, which is subject to a binding purchase and sale agreement at the time of death, the doctrine of equitable conversion applies, and the asset of the estate is the right to the proceeds, not the real estate.

An exception to the ademption rule is if the testator's conservator or guardian sold the property.

In that example, the beneficiary is entitled to anything that remains of the proceeds of the sale.

Pecuniary bequests – ademption by satisfaction

If the testator gives a prospective legatee a gift before the will is executed, that gift will not be considered to have satisfied a bequest.

If a gift is received by a beneficiary from the testator after the will is executed, it will only be considered to have satisfied the bequest if the testator declared in writing that it was in satisfaction of the gift or unless the beneficiary acknowledged in writing that the gift was in satisfaction of the bequest.

The rule is like that of advancements for intestate shares.

Changes in securities

A legatee is only entitled to the number of shares of the security as has been bequeathed to them, providing that the testator owned that many shares at death.

The legatee is entitled to additional shares of security if the testator received them as a stock split or stock dividend from the original shares bequeathed.

The specific legatee is entitled to securities received in exchange for the bequeathed securities due to a merger, consolidation, reorganization, or similar action.

Encumbered property

The devisee of real property or the legatee of personal property takes the property subject to any mortgage or security interest at the time of death unless the will provides differently.

Lapse – changes in beneficiaries

Unless the will provides an alternative disposition if the named beneficiary predeceases the testator or unless the anti-lapse statute applies, a legacy or devise made to one who predeceases the testator lapses.

If the lapsed legacy is not a residuary, the amount of that legacy becomes part of the estate's residue and passes under the residuary clause.

If the lapsed legacy is the residuary legacy, the assets pass by intestacy.

The anti-lapse statute

When an anti-lapse statute is applicable, the legacy which was supposed to go to a deceased beneficiary is transferred to the issue of that deceased beneficiary provided that the testator has not shown a different intent.

The anti-lapse statute is only applicable when the deceased beneficiary is a blood relative of the testator.

A gift to the deceased child of a spouse does not pass by operation of the anti-lapse statute to the issue of that child.

For the anti-lapse statute to operate, the deceased relative must have been survived by issue, including adopted children.

The property passes to the issue per the law of intestate distribution discussed above.

For example, if the beneficiary were survived by two children and the two children of a deceased child, the children take one-third of the legacy. The remaining one-third would be split between the children of the deceased child.

The legacy is not paid under the will of the deceased relation.

If the deceased blood relative survived by issue dies before the execution of the will, the anti-lapse statute will still apply.

If there are two or more residuary legatees and one predeceases the testator, the remaining legatees take the residue, and nothing is distributed by intestacy.

If the deceased residuary legatee is a relation and is survived by issue, the anti-lapse statute applies, and the issue takes the deceased residuary legatee's share of the residue.

Class gifts – definition of a class

A class gift exists when a testator makes a gift to several persons, usually with the same relationship to the testator, such as "nephews and nieces."

The class may increase in number as additional persons are born and qualify as members of the class, or it may decrease as members of the class die before the time the gift is to be distributed.

Whether a group of beneficiaries is to be considered a class or to be considered individually is answered by determining the intent of the testator.

Time to determine membership

If the class gift is a legacy or devise to be paid at the time of the testator's death, membership in the class is determined at the testator's death.

Persons who have predeceased the testator, even if they were alive at the time of the will, are not members of the class.

Even if they bear an appropriate relationship to become class members, persons born after the testator's death are excluded.

If the class gift is payable at some time after the testator's death, the time for determining membership in the class is the time when the property is distributed to the class.

Unless there is a provision in the will that conditions the benefits of the class gift upon survivorship until distribution time, membership in the class does not decrease after the testator's death. However, it can increase with births after death but before distribution.

If distribution of the benefits of the class gift takes place over time (e.g., beneficiaries are eligible for distributions when they obtain a specific age), the rule of convenience, which can be overcome by expressing a contrary intent, closes class membership at the first distribution.

The anti-lapse applies to class gifts.

If the testator left the property 'to my brother for life and his children," the statute allows the issue of the testator's nephews and nieces who predeceased the testator to take.

However, if the provision were "to my brother for life and then to his children then living," the anti-lapse statute could not apply because there is a condition of survivorship.

Changes in marital status – marriage

Marriage after the date of the execution of the will revokes an entire will unless it appears from the will itself that it was made in contemplation of the marriage.

Unless such a testator makes a new will after marriage, their estate is distributed by intestacy laws.

A will revoked by marriage is not revived by divorce.

Changes in marital status – divorce

A divorce or annulment revokes provisions in a will for the former spouse, and the property passes as if the former spouse had predeceased the testator.

A divorce revokes the designation of the former spouse in a fiduciary capacity under the will.

If the testator remarries their former spouse, the provisions are revived.

A legal separation of spouses does not terminate their married status and does not revoke any provisions of a will.

Community property

States such as Arizona, California, Idaho, Louisiana, Nevada, New Mexico, Texas, Washington, and Wisconsin recognize a form of co-ownership known as community property. This method of co-ownership applies only to married couples and is based on the notion that a husband and wife should share equally in the fruits of the marital partnership. Under these laws, each spouse owns an equal half share of the income of both spouses and the assets acquired during the marriage regardless of who earns the income. Property acquired through gift or inheritance before or during the marriage remains separate property. When a spouse dies, the surviving spouse automatically receives one-half the community property.

The other half passes to the deceased spouse's heirs as directed by the will or by state intestate statute if there is no will. Neither spouse can sell, transfer, or gift community property during the marriage without the other spouse's consent.

Upon divorce, each spouse has a right to one-half of the community property. The location of the real property determines whether community property law applies. For example, if a married couple who lives in a noncommunity property state purchases real property located in a community property state, community property laws apply to that property.

Notes for active learning

The Distribution of The Estate After Death

The estate at the time of death

Most exam questions require explaining how the estate of the decedent is distributed at death.

The will, which was ambulatory until the time of death, becomes an operative instrument by the process of probate.

A petition to probate the decedent's last will and testament is filed by the executor in the probate (e.g., county) court of the decedent's domicile at the time of death.

The burden of proving that the will was validly executed, that it has not been revoked, and that the decedent was competent at the time of execution is on the proponent of the will.

The decree admitting the will to probate established the will as the decedent's probate estate's dispositive instrument.

The decree may be revoked if a later will is found or the will was a forgery.

The named executor is ordinarily appointed executor when the will is allowed, but the court has the discretion to appoint a different fiduciary if the named executor is unfit.

If there is no will, the probate process is known as administration.

The surviving spouse has the first claim on the fiduciary position of the administrator.

Children have the next right to the appointment as administrators.

The administrator performs duties like an executor and distributes the estate following the laws of intestacy.

Will contests

The decedent's heirs and beneficiaries of a prior will have standing to contest the validity of the will offered for probate on one or more of three grounds.

The heirs must be given notice of the petition for probate.

Legatees under prior wills should be given notice if their existence is known, but failure to notice prior legatees will not void the probate proceeding.

A testator may include a valid and enforceable provision in their will requiring any legatee who contests the will to forfeit any provisions made under the will.

A beneficiary petition for interpretation of a will does not challenge the validity of the will and therefore does not invoke an *in terrorem* clause.

Improper execution

If the will was improperly executed, it is invalid.

Improper execution will occur if the testator fails to sign the will in the presence of witnesses or acknowledge to them that the signature on the will is theirs or the statutory number of witnesses (e.g., one, two) fail to attest to the will.

The named executor has the burden of proving proper execution.

Lack of testamentary capacity

The validity of the will may be challenged if the decedent was under age 18 when the will was executed or if they were not of sound mind.

The burden is on the proponents to establish a sound mind once those challenging the will have produced credible evidence of an unsound mind.

Undue influence

A ground for challenging the will is that the testator was under undue influence at execution.

To constitute undue influence, coercion (mental, physical, or moral) must cause the desires of the person accused of using undue influence to be incorporated into the will rather than the desires of the testator.

Kindness or care for the decedent does not constitute undue influence if the testator responds by giving such person a substantial legacy.

If the person accused of exerting undue influence is in a fiduciary relationship to the testator and benefits themself, the court will likely find undue influence.

Legacies in favor of the scrivener of the will are particularly suspect.

The contestant bears the burden of proving undue influence.

Fraud in the inducement

Fraud, which deprives the testator of their right to make a will based upon the true state of affairs, is of two types, fraud in the inducement and fraud in the factum.

Fraud in the inducement is a knowingly false representation that causes the testator to make a different will than otherwise.

If successfully proven, fraud in the inducement will only void those provisions of the will, which were the product of that fraud, and the remaining portions of the will can be probated.

If the testator, in the absence of fraud, makes a mistake not having to do with the execution of the will, which induces them to dispose of property in a particular manner, the will is valid.

For example, a mistake about the value of one's property, or concerning how the decedent has been treated by one of their relatives, or whether the natural object of one's bounty is living or dead will not invalidate the will.

The test for determining whether the testator had sufficient mental capacity to create a valid trust is typically like that required to make a valid will. To have capacity, the settlor must have been at least 18 years old and must know the extent of their property and the natural objects of their bounty. The "natural objects" include family members such as spouses, children, and siblings.

Fraud in the *factum*

Fraud in the factum occurs when the decedent is defrauded that they are making a will or about the contents of the will.

For example, the decedent thinks they are signing a contract when the document is a will, or the decedent signs a will but does not know that there are beneficiaries in the will whom they did not want.

For it to be the basis to contest a will, the fraud must be operative when the will was executed.

The burden of proving fraud is on the contestant.

Fraud in the *factum* goes to whether the decedent knew that they were executing a will and voids the instrument.

Remedies for fraud and undue influence

A person objecting to a will based on fraud or undue influence must contest the validity of the will in probate and cannot maintain a separate action for constructive trust or tort damages.

If the fraud or undue influence prevented the execution of a will in favor of the plaintiff, they would maintain a tort action for interference with an advantageous relationship.

If the alleged wrongdoer benefited from their conduct by taking under the decedent's will, the remedy for the person who was left out of the will is to ask the court to impose a *constructive trust* upon the defendant's ill-gotten gains for the plaintiff's benefit.

A constructive trust is not an actual trust by the traditional definition; a constructive trust is a legal fiction remedy for unjust enrichment.

The constructive trust orders the unjustly enriched person to transfer the property to the intended party.

Other reasons for the invalidity of a will

The probate court, where the will is probated, is the forum to address other issues concerning the validity of the will, such as whether the will has been revoked or terminated by a subsequent marriage.

If the court determines that a will is invalid for any reason, prior wills may be probated since the provision in the invalid will revoking prior wills is invalid.

If there are no prior wills, the court treats the probate as an administration and distributes property by the laws of intestacy.

Issues altering the operation of the will

The probate court is the forum where the issues of pretermitted children and waiver of the will by a surviving spouse are determined.

Collection of the assets of the estate

Once appointed, the executor or administrator collects the estate assets and files an inventory.

Special rules affect the following assets.

Debts owed by the executor to the estate

Any debt which the executor owes to the estate is treated as paid.

The executor must account for that money in their final account.

If the executor cannot pay it and they filed a surety bond, the sureties must pay the amount the executor owed the estate.

Income from specifically bequeathed assets

Income-producing assets specifically devised or bequeathed carry the right to income from the date of death.

The executor is entitled to the income accrued to the decedent before death as a general asset of the estate.

Income accruing after death is paid to the beneficiaries of the specifically bequeathed assets.

Real estate – heirs or devisees normally have control

Real estate descends directly to the heirs or devisees, and the executor does not have the right to rents nor the responsibilities of management as soon as the will is allowed.

Executor may sell real estate to pay debts and expenses

If the estate's personal property assets are insufficient to pay debts and taxes of the estate, the executor has the power to petition the probate court to sell real estate to satisfy obligations.

To give good title to real estate during the first year after the death, a license from the probate court for the executor to sell with the assent of the devisees is necessary.

Powers and duties of a fiduciary

Unless the will or a probate court order confers greater authority, the executor or administrator has limited power.

The executor may expend money to protect and preserve estate assets and comply with the decedent's contractual obligations.

To liquidate the estate, the executor has the power to sell personal property.

If the estate is solvent, the executor or administrator can keep the assets that the decedent held and distribute assets in kind or partly in kind.

Standard of executor's obligations

An executor or administrator is a fiduciary and subject to fiduciary duties of care and loyalty

Liability of executor or administrator

An executor is not personally liable for contracts made by them in their capacity as an executor unless they failed to reveal their fiduciary capacity.

A creditor may hold the estate liable on such contracts.

The estate, but not the executor, is liable in tort due to control of the estate's property unless the executor is personally negligent.

To satisfy the duty of care, an executor must carry liability insurance on managed property.

Payment of debts and claims

The executor or administrator first uses the estate assets to pay debts and claims in the following order of priority.

A widow's allowance (payable immediately after death without regard to the estate's debts) to help the widow and minor children adjust to death has priority on the assets.

The amount is per minor child given with a limited amount for necessaries for the widow.

A widower would probably qualify for such an allowance.

The priorities for debts are in the following order:

1) expenses of administration;

2) necessary funeral expenses and expenses of last illness;

3) debts entitled to preference under laws of the United States;

4) taxes and excise duties;

5) wages (up to statutory amount) for labor performed within a year of death;

6) debts for necessaries furnished to the decedent or their family within 6 months of death;

7) all other debts.

If the assets are insufficient to satisfy one class in full, the debts abate pro-rata.

Priority of secured debts with collateral

A secured party, including a mortgagee, may seek repayment out of the security and is not subject to priorities except the extent to which the debt exceeds the collateral value.

Suits for services – claimant can testify

Since some states have no dead man rule, plaintiffs can testify to an oral contract with the deceased for services.

If the claim is for services rendered, only claims accruing during the last six years of the decedent's life are collectible because of the statute of limitations.

Claim to leave property by will

If the claim is that services were rendered in reliance on an oral promise to leave the property by will, the suit on the contract to leave the property by will is unenforceable because of the statute of frauds.

The plaintiff can sue the estate and collect damages in *quantum meruit* for the fair value of services rendered in reliance on the unenforceable oral promise.

The cause of action for a promise to leave the property by will does not accrue until the will becomes operative at the time of death.

The contract statute of limitations will not bar a claim for services rendered in reliance on the promise, and the plaintiff can collect for services rendered after the date of the promise if the estate is sued promptly.

Debts due to the executor

If the executor has a claim against the estate, they may collect it.

The beneficiaries have a right to contest the validity and amount under arbitration procedures established by the probate court.

Notice of claim filed against an estate

A creditor should make a claim by mailing a written statement of the claim to the executor within the statutory period (e.g., four months) after the executor or administrator has been appointed, describing the nature and extent of the claim.

Disallowance of claims

The executor or administrator has a statutory period (e.g., sixty days) after receipt to disallow the claim.

Failure to disallow gives that claim the status of an allowed claim and tolls the statute of limitations for suits against estates.

Payments during the statutory period

Because the executor or administrator does not know the number of claims against an estate, the executor should not pay claims within the statutory period (e.g., four months) from their appointment.

If the executor pays claims they have knowledge of after the statutory period, they are not personally liable to creditors who make a later claim, which would render the estate insolvent.

Statute of limitations for suits against the estate

Suits against the estate, except for the exceptions discussed hereafter, must be brought within the statutory period from the deceased's death.

Notes for active learning

Exceptions to One-Year Statute for Suits Against the Estate

The Supreme Court may permit a late-filed claim if it finds the claimant is not guilty of culpable neglect and that equity and justice require the waiver.

New assets in an estate

If new assets come into the estate more than one year after the decedent's death, creditors may sue for the new assets within six months after the executor receives them or four months after the creditor learns of them, whichever comes first.

Claim not yet accrued

If a claim is presented before the estate is fully administered but will not accrue during the one year, the court may order that sufficient assets be held to satisfy the claim when it matures, and the lawsuit need not be commenced until the cause of action accrues.

Claim satisfied out of insurance

If the claim is to be satisfied by an insurance policy or bond, the suit may be brought within the time limits of the ordinary statute of limitations if that suit is within three years of the date of death.

Tax returns

The executor is responsible for paying the federal estate tax and filing estate tax returns if the estate is large enough to require that a return be filed.

The executor must file fiduciary income tax returns to report the income earned by the estate.

Notes for active learning

Payment of Legacies and Distributive Shares

Payment to a spouse in intestacy without issue

The administrator must pay a statutory amount to the spouse first out of personalty and then from the realty in an intestate administration where a spouse, but no issue survives.

If the entire net probate estate is less than the statutory amount, the administrator can obtain a determination that the surviving spouse is entitled to the entire estate.

Time of the payment of legacies

Legacies are not payable until a statutory period (e.g., nine months) after the executor's appointment.

General or pecuniary legacies carry interest after the statutory period elapses.

A legacy to support a minor or widow instead of a dower bears interest from the date of death.

Income earned from the date of death from a bequeathed asset is paid to that beneficiary.

Legacies to executor, debtors, and creditors

A legacy to a person named as an executor ordinarily requires that the executor serves in that capacity to qualify for the legacy.

Whether a bequest left to a creditor of the estate is used to reduce the debt owed is determined by the intent of the testator.

The size of the bequest, the relationship between the creditor and testator, the character of the legacy, and the time the debt arose are relevant factors in making that determination.

If the testator is a creditor of the legatee, the executor has the right to offset the debt against the legacy unless the legatee shows that the testator intended to forgive the debt and grant a legacy.

If the statute of limitations barred the debt at the time of the execution of the will, there is a strong indication that the testator did not intend that it be collected.

Abatement of legacies

The testator has the power to specify the order in which legacies will abate where the assets are insufficient.

If the assets of the estate are insufficient to pay the creditors and legacies in the will, the order of abatement is:

1) residuary legacies;

2) general legacies which abate *pro-rata* if not enough assets exclusive of specific legacies to pay them in full;

3) specific legacies and devises that abate pro-rata if specific legacies and devises must be used to satisfy the estate's debts.

Legacies satisfying a legal obligation of 1) the testator, 2) a minor, 3) instead of dower, or 4) as the result of an ante-nuptial agreement, are entitled to priority over specific legacies and devises.

Completion of the Administration of the Estate

Filing account

Upon complete administration of the estate, the executor or administrator files a final account, showing inventory, income, expenses, and distributions.

Challenge to account

Heirs and other interested persons have a right to challenge the account.

If found deficient, the executor can be required to pay sums into the estate, and the sureties can be held liable if the executor defaults.

Finality of account

Once allowed, the executor is discharged and is subject to further challenge only if the allowance of the account was procured by fraud or manifest error.

Notes for active learning

Domicile

The domicile determines intestate succession to personal property.

If the will is in writing and is signed, a will executed in conformity with either the law of the testator's domicile or the law of the place where it was executed will be recognized as a valid will by state court.

If the decedent who executed a will out of state dies domiciled in the state, the construction and legal effect of a disposition of personalty are governed by state law; and the disposition of real estate is governed by the law of its *situs* of that real estate.

A choice-of-law provision in a will specifying that a specific state's law will govern it will be recognized unless the law of a different state is contrary to public policy.

The decedent is most familiar with the laws of their domicile.

Attorney consultations would most likely be conducted in the domicile.

The domicile state bears the burden of intestate distribution.

The domicile of the decedent is used to choose the law to be applied to determine the intestate succession of personal property.

Domicile at death determines which state gets estate taxes.

The law of the *situs* determines intestate succession to real property.

Conflicting domicile determinations – the states apply their standards for determining domicile and may separately rule that a party was domiciled in their respective state (a legal impossibility).

Dorrance v Martin et al. (1935) – two states imposed estate taxes after deciding that the decedent was domiciled in their respective state.

The imposition of multiple state estate taxes violates the due process clause only if the taxes exceed the value of the estate. To avoid additional tax, an intent to change domiciles should be done thoroughly and quickly.

Choice of laws application

For land, the law of the *situs* applies.

Movable property – law of the *situs,* but issues arise (e.g., the *situs* of stock certificate).

Personal property – the domicile of the decedent at death.

The policy governs the status of property *vs.* determining who takes under a will (*situs* rule fractionalizes estate but might be consistent with expectations).

For wills, it might be better to look at domicile at the time of execution.

Intestate succession is determined by domicile. Domicile is determined by the law of the forum and requires physical presence and intent to remain indefinitely.

Modern rule – domicile depends on the issue (old rule: unitary).

White v. Tennant (WV 1888) (moved from PA to WV but for less than one day): domicile was established upon arrival.

Estate of Jones (Iowa 1921) (Lusitania): death in transit uses the previous domicile until "new domicile is secured."

Model Execution of Wills Act, which provides that the testator will subscribe to a written document shall be valid as to matters of the form if it complies with the local requirements of several enumerated states.

Definition of a Trust

Trusts divide legal and equitable interests

A trust is an entity recognized by the law in which a trustee holds legal title to the property to benefit the beneficiaries who have an equitable interest in the trust property.

Separation of the legal and equitable title is an essential element of a trust.

If a sole trustee who holds the legal interest is identical to the sole beneficiary holding the equitable interests, there is a merger.

The trust is terminated, and the sole trustee/beneficiary owns the property outright.

An essential element of a trust is that the trustee stands in a fiduciary relationship with the beneficiaries concerning the trust property.

Distinguished from other relationships

Agency, debtor-creditor, and bailment distinguish between trust and other legal relationships.

The facts may be ambiguous in some questions, so discuss the law of trusts and analyze the facts under one of the following legal frameworks.

Agency

A trust is distinguished from an agency because an agent does not hold legal title to the principal's property.

Debtor–creditor

A trust is not a debtor–creditor relationship.

A creditor has a claim at law against the debtor for damages in the amount of the debt. In contrast, a trust beneficiary has an equitable interest in specific trust property and the benefit of the trustee's fiduciary obligations.

Bailment

A bailee only has a possessory interest, not title, in the property held for the bailee.

While the bailee has a duty to avoid negligence concerning the property and can be required to turn the property over to the bailor, there is no fiduciary duty between the bailor and bailee.

Notes for active learning

Voluntarily Created Trusts

Methods of trust creation

A voluntary trust is created when the settlor with the express or implied intent to create a trust performs the acts necessary to establish a trust.

The acts of the settlor may be donative or required by a contractual relationship.

The act which accompanies the creation of a trust is a *declaration* or *transfer*.

Trust creation by declaration

A trust is created by a declaration when the settler, orally or in writing, intends to hold property that they own in trust and hold it at least partially for others' benefit.

When a declaration creates a trust, the settlor is the trustee, and the settlor holds legal title to the property in their fiduciary capacity as trustee.

Trust creation by transfer

A trust can be created when the settlor transfers the legal title to their property to a third party and designates the beneficiaries who have the equitable title to the property.

Voluntary or donative trusts

A voluntary trust is created without consideration by declaration (or transfer).

A declaration needs communication of the intent to hold property in trust and does not need to comply with the formalities of a transfer.

Thus, an individual can make an effective gift in trust by declaring that they are holding property, which they own in trust, for the benefit of the donee of the gift without the need of delivery to complete the gift.

If a transfer is necessary to complete the creation of a voluntary trust, the settlor must comply with the delivery requirements for a donative transaction to be complete.

Personal property must be delivered to the trustee.

There must be execution and delivery of a deed to the trustee for a trust to be created by the transfer of real property

A voluntary declaration of trust requires a clear showing of intent to create a trust.

If the declaration of trust is oral, there must be notice to and acceptance by the beneficiary.

No notice to a beneficiary is needed with a written declaration of trust.

Trusts created by contract

If there is an obligation to create a trust by a contract supported by valid consideration and that obligation is specifically enforceable, the person who has agreed to create a trust can be required in equity to satisfy their obligation and transfer the property to a trust.

If the promise involves a trust where the *res* (body) of the trust is land, the contract will have to be enforceable under the statute of frauds.

Testamentary or *inter vivos* trusts

A testamentary trust is created in a will and becomes operational only at death.

An *inter vivos* trust becomes effective during the lifetime of the settlor.

Pour-over provisions for testamentary trusts

A trust created by the terms of a will is only valid if the will is valid and can only be amended by a subsequent will or a codicil.

Under the doctrine of incorporation by reference, the estate assets may be bequeathed or devised to an existing inter-vivos trust.

This trust is known as a pour-over trust.

By statute, if the trust is in existence when the will is executed, the trust can subsequently be amended by the testator in a manner that does not observe the formalities of executing a will. The assets poured into the trust will be governed by the terms of the amended trust.

An *inter vivos* trust is irrevocable unless the settlor expressly retained the power to revoke it.

If a settlor attempts to set up a trust that will only come into existence at their death, it must be created by an instrument executed with the formalities of a will.

If the trust is created during the lifetime of the testator, it will not be invalid because it did not comply with the formalities of wills even if the settlor is the sole trustee, the sole lifetime beneficiary, and retains the power to amend and revoke it.

Such a trust is the classic pour-over trust commonly used today.

Savings account trust

A common substitute for a testamentary disposition is a savings bank trust where the donor opens an account in their name in trust for the donee.

There must be a formal document setting forth the terms of the trust, or the donor must give notice to the beneficiary that the trust has been created.

Gifts to minors

The Transfers to Minors Act allows the registration of certain types of personal property in a custodian's name for a minor.

The custodian may make payments for the minor's use and benefit without court approval, and the property becomes the sole property of the minor upon reaching majority.

Notes for active learning

Required Elements of a Trust

For a private voluntary trust to be validly created, the following elements are necessary

Once created, a trust will not fail for lack of a trustee because the courts can always appoint a successor trustee if no trustee is named in the instrument.

Capacity of the settlor

The settlor must be of sufficient age and mental capacity.

If the trust is testamentary, the validity of the trust depends upon the validity of the will.

The capacity of the testator/settlor can be challenged in a will contest.

The creation of an *inter vivos* trust requires a present capacity of the settlor to declare that they are holding property in trust or conveying the trust property.

The settlor must convey the present intent to create a trust relationship where the legal title to the property is held by a trustee for the benefit of a beneficiary and must comply with the formalities of creating a trust by declaring themselves trustee or transferring the property to a trustee.

To create a trust, the language employed by the transferor settlor when transferring the property to a transferee must impose mandatory obligations on the transferee to hold the property in trust for the benefit of the trust beneficiaries.

If the transferor uses precatory language such as "wish," "hope," "request," or "desire" for the transferee's use of the property, they will not create a trust due to the lack of an enforceable obligation placed upon the transferee.

Where the circumstances show that the settlor did intend to impose mandatory duties, a court may construe precatory language as creating mandatory obligations on the transferee and therefore creating a trust.

In making that determination, the court may be more likely to find a trust if the settlor had an obligation to support the beneficiaries.

Necessity for writing

A testamentary trust is part of a will and must always be created by formally executed writings.

An *inter vivos* trust may be created orally if it involves only personal property.

An *inter vivos* trust containing land created by a settlor's declaration is valid only if the settlor has executed a writing indicating that they are holding the land in trust.

If the trust in land is created by transfer to the trustee, that transfer must be in writing.

If a purported settlor conveys land to a third person without indication that the third person holds the property in a trust, the transferee can carry out the terms of the trust that were given by the trustee orally or void any trust obligation.

An oral promise to hold proceeds from the sale of land in a trust is not within the Statute of Frauds and will be enforced when the trustee sells the property.

Trust property

There must be some identifiable trust property in which the settlor can declare that they hold in trust or with a present right to convey to a trustee.

Intangible property interests and contingent interests, which are more than mere expectancy, can be the subject of a trust.

Definite or ascertainable beneficiaries

For a private trust instead of a charitable trust discussed later, the beneficiaries must be identified or ascertainable.

The settlor may designate a definite and ascertainable class of persons as beneficiaries.

Valid trust purpose

A private express trust cannot be created for an illegal purpose or contrary to public policy.

If the trustee, in carrying out the terms of the trust, would be required to commit a tortious act or defraud creditors of the settlor, the trust is invalid.

Time restrictions

The Uniform Statutory Rule Against Perpetuities provides that the interest of the beneficiaries in the principal of a trust, or a special, testamentary, or contingent power of appointment is valid if it is certain to vest within the common-law rule period or does vest within 90 years after its creation.

The statute embodies a wait rule, which allows the non-vested property interest a grace period of 90 years to vest.

The statute has a reformation provision that allows a court on the petition of an "interested person" to modify an invalid disposition under the rule stated above so that it follows the grantor's intent as nearly as possible but does, in fact, vest within 90 years.

Defining Characteristics of Charitable Trusts

Charitable purpose

A legally recognized charitable purpose, such as the furtherance of health, religion, education, government, or the arts, is an essential characteristic of a charitable trust.

The settlor can create a charitable trust that does not set forth a defined charitable purpose but limits the trustees' activity to the furtherance of charitable purposes.

Indefinite class of beneficiaries

For a trust to qualify as charitable, there must be a public benefit, so the persons to be benefited must be members of an indefinite class.

If a defined class of beneficiaries such as a scholarship trust at a university for the settlor's descendants, the trust is not charitable.

If the class of beneficiaries is large such as the inhabitants of a specific town, the indefinite class of beneficiaries' test has been met.

Similarities to private trusts

A charitable trust may be created by any methods for creating an express trust, and there must be a settlor with the capacity to convey properly expressed intent, and a specific trust *res* (or *corpus*), and power of enforcement.

Notes for active learning

Limitations of Private Trusts Inapplicable to Charitable Trusts

Rule against perpetuities inapplicable

A charitable trust may continue indefinitely and is not subject to the rule against perpetuities or the rule against accumulations unless the accumulation is found to be unreasonable.

Failure of purpose

When some other change in circumstances renders it impracticable to administer the trust as provided by the settlor, or the charitable purpose intended by the settlor has or can no longer be accomplished, the doctrine of *cy pres* (as near as possible) may be applicable.

Instead of terminating the trust, the courts alter the trust's purpose to continue while following the settlor's original intent as possible.

Under the *cy pres* doctrine (i.e.., *amending a legal document*), a court may modify the trust's purpose and permit the trustee to use the trust *res* (body) for another charitable purpose, close to the settlor's original charitable intent.

If the trust instrument indicates that the *cy pres* doctrine is not applied, the trust *res* (i.e., body) reverts to the settlor or their estate.

Enforcing the trust

In a private trust, the beneficiaries have the power to enforce the provisions of the trust.

Since there are no defined beneficiaries in a charitable trust, the enforcement power is given by statute to the state's Attorney General.

Notes for active learning

Spendthrift Provisions

Protections for beneficiaries

A beneficiary's equitable interest in income or principal of the trust may be voluntarily assigned and may be subjected to the claims of judgment creditors of the beneficiary unless the terms of the trust provide otherwise.

The settlor may insert a spendthrift provision in a trust, which validly prohibits the beneficiary from transferring their interest in the trust before it is distributed to them.

Such a provision prevents the beneficiary's creditors from reaching the beneficiary's interest in the trust to satisfy their claims.

Once a beneficiary receives a distribution from the trust, creditors may reach that distribution.

A settlor cannot insert a spendthrift provision in a trust which protects their beneficial interest in the trust from creditors.

A discretionary trust, in which the beneficiary has no right to income until the trustee decides to pay it, will so protect the beneficiary's interest from creditors.

The settlor can give the trustee the discretionary power to pay income due to a specific beneficiary or accumulate it and provide that the trustee has the discretion to pay the income among several beneficiaries.

When those provisions are in place, neither the beneficiary nor their creditors can compel payment or funds from the trust.

Notes for active learning

Administration of the Trust by the Trustee

Appointment of the trustee

The settlor ordinarily has the power to select the trustee and provide for succession of trustees.

If the trustee refuses to serve or fails to qualify, the probate court has broad discretion in naming a trustee or appointing a successor trustee to fill a vacancy.

Resignation or removal of the trustee

Once a trustee is in office, they may resign if authorized by the trust instrument or with permission of all the beneficiaries or the probate court.

The probate court has the power to remove a trustee upon a petition filed by the beneficiaries for failing to perform their duties, breaching a fiduciary duty, or where there is hostility between the trustee and the beneficiaries.

Compensation of the trustee

A trustee is entitled to receive reasonable compensation for their services as a trustee.

A trustee is entitled to reimbursement for expenses occurring in the administration of the trust.

A trustee who is an attorney can render legal services to the trust and be paid separately for those services.

If the trust instrument does not allocate fees between income and principal, the court can determine the allocation.

Notes for active learning

Powers of the Trustee

The trustee has powers conferred by the trust instrument to manage the trust assets and distribute them to beneficiaries; the trustee may incorporate statutory optional fiduciary powers by reference.

Power of sale or contract

Without a specific grant of power, a trustee may sell and transfer personal property unless the trust instrument prohibits such sale.

The authority to sell or transfer real estate must be expressly granted in the trust.

Otherwise, the trust must obtain court approval to sell or transfer real estate.

A trustee has the power to enter contracts on behalf of the trust and further has the power to execute instruments that will accomplish or facilitate the exercise of their other powers.

Power to invest

A trustee has the power and duty to invest the trust property, make the property productive, and use reasonable care and skill to choose and manage investments.

Power of apportionment

If the trust provides that income is paid to one set of beneficiaries and principal to another set, the trust instrument sets the standards for apportionment of income and expenses.

Absent authority in the trust instrument, the trustee should pay ordinary expenses out of income and extraordinary expenses and those solely beneficial to the remainder interests out of principal.

The general rule provides that cash dividends are allocated to income and stock dividends to the principal.

Power to invade principal

The trust instrument can provide discretionary principal payments to income beneficiaries and usually set up a standard by which such payments should be made.

The discretion of the trustee to make such payments will rarely be disturbed by a court.

Unless there is power in the trust instrument to invade principal, a court will not permit principal payments to an income beneficiary if the instrument benefits a different principal beneficiary.

If an income beneficiary is the sole principal beneficiary upon a particular age, the court has the discretion to permit principal payment acceleration for circumstances not foreseen by the settlor.

Duties and Liabilities of the Trustee

Duty of loyalty and good faith

The highest fiduciary duty of loyalty is imposed upon a trustee.

The trustee must avoid conflicts of interest between their interests and the trusts and between the interests of others to whom the trustee owes a fiduciary duty and those of the trust.

When a conflict occurs, the trustee cannot enter a transaction on behalf of the trust unless the transaction is fair to the trust and the trust instrument authorizes them explicitly, or the trustee makes appropriate disclosure and receives permission from the court or beneficiaries.

If a beneficiary is not competent to act, guardian *ad litem* should be appointed and act on behalf of the incompetent beneficiaries.

If the trustee takes an action that affects life tenants and remaindermen, the trustee must act fairly to each group.

If the trustee purchases property in their individual capacity, which is an appropriate opportunity for the trust, a constructive trust can be imposed upon the property held by the trustee in their individual capacity.

A constructive trust can be imposed upon the property if the trustee purchases property from the trust without complying with their fiduciary obligations.

Duty of reasonable care and skill

The trustee must abide by the limitations imposed by the trust instrument for their powers of investment.

The trustee must exercise reasonable care and skill in managing the trust.

The trust instrument can authorize the trustee to take greater risks with trust investments and particularly authorize the trustee to retain the investments transferred initially to the trust even though the investment concentration would not be prudent for trust investment.

If the trustee exercises the required standard of care, they are not liable for mistakes in judgment.

Unless the trust instrument authorizes delegation explicitly, a trustee may not delegate their duties to others, except for ministerial (i.e., purely administrative) duties.

Even though a trustee can seek expert advice on matters concerning trust property, the trustee must supervise agents and make the final decision on actions suggested.

Trust property must not be commingled with the trustee's property.

Except when there is an authority to invest in a common trust fund, it should not be placed with funds from other trusts.

Duty to make property productive

The trustee may not keep unproductive property such as vacant land as an asset of the trust unless the trust instrument authorizes this or the beneficiary's consent for such an investment.

The trustee has a duty to sell the unproductive property and reinvest in productive assets.

Duty to account

The trustee has a duty to account to the beneficiaries, telling them how they managed the trust property, the income they are entitled to, and the amount of principal held in the trust.

Liability to third parties

A trustee is not personally liable for a contract, which they make in a disclosed capacity as a trust unless the contract expressly provides personal liability.

A trustee is not personally liable for torts committed during prudent administration of the trust unless there is a personal fault by the trustee.

The trust estate is liable for claims in tort or contract for obligations entered by the trustee or tort claims arising from the trust's property.

Termination of the Trust

Termination by the settlor

The settlor's unilateral action could terminate a trust if they reserved the power in the trust instrument to revoke it.

If the power is not reserved, the trust cannot be terminated by the settlor unless they obtain all the beneficiaries' consent, which must be of legal age and competent.

Termination after the settlor's death

Even if all the beneficiaries of a trust approve of its termination after the settlor's death, courts will not ordinarily terminate it before the time specified in the trust if such termination is contrary to the settlor's intent.

Where no material purpose of the settlor remains to be accomplished, the court may allow termination upon request of all the beneficiaries whose interests are vested and who are competent to consent.

If the trust is spendthrift or discretionary, the settlor's purpose in creating the trust has not been fulfilled, so it cannot be terminated even if all the beneficiaries desire such termination.

The trustee has no power to terminate the trust unless such power was expressly granted.

If the trustee has the power to distribute the principal of the trust, they can effectively terminate it by conveying the trust property to the beneficiaries per the terms of the trust.

Termination by the court

If an emergency or unforeseen circumstance (e.g., severe medical need) by a beneficiary causes the trust purpose to be impaired or frustrated, a court may terminate the trust even though the settlor's material purpose still exists, and beneficiaries do not consent.

Notes for active learning

Trusts Created by Operation of Law

There are two kinds of legal entities labeled as trusts, purchase money *resulting trusts* and *constructive trusts* created by operation of law, and do not fit the classic definition of trusts.

Each entity is important for exam purposes because candidates must be aware of the circumstances where they are operative and discuss them in their answers.

Resulting trusts – failure or inadequacy of express trust

If the settlor failed to create an express trust and has transferred the property to an individual whom they intended to act as a trustee or the settlor has transferred the property to the trustee above that needed to accomplish the purposes of the trust, that person holds the property for the settlor, heirs, or successors.

The trust is a resulting trust because it is presumed that, upon the failure of an express trust or the lack of need, the settlor intended the property be retained for their benefit.

If a trust were created because of a contractual obligation of the settlor, the trust could fail.

If the person intended to be benefited by the contractual obligation creating a trust becomes the legal owner of the property rather than a beneficiary, no resulting trust was created.

If the settlor used precatory language when they transferred property, so no trust exists, and the transferee of the property holds the property outright, and no resulting trust exists.

Purchase money conveyances

When one person pays consideration for the transfer of property, but the title is taken in the name of another person, and there is no donative intent on the part of the person paying the consideration, the person receiving the property holds it in a purchase money resulting trust.

If the person named who furnished the consideration has an obligation to support the person whose name title is taken, the presumption for a gift and no resulting trust arises.

The presumption of a gift arises where one spouse furnishes the consideration for the purchased property, and the title is taken in the name of the other spouse.

No such presumption of a gift occurs if a parent furnishes the consideration and title is taken in the name of an adult child

Even where there is a presumption of a gift, that presumption may be rebutted by clear and convincing evidence, and a resulting trust arises.

The statute of frauds does not apply to a resulting trust.

Proof of the intent not to make a gift and not to vest a beneficial interest in the grantee of the deed may be made by parol evidence.

A resulting trust must arise at the time of purchase from a third party.

If the person furnishing the consideration takes the title from the seller in their name and subsequently transfers property upon an oral promise of the grantee to hold the property in trust, no resulting trust is presumed.

If the person who did not take title paid only part of the purchase price, they might establish a resulting trust for a partial interest in the property if they show clear and convincing evidence that their payment was for a distinct interest in the property.

Constructive trusts

A court creates a constructive trust as an equitable remedy when there is no intention (express or presumed) to create a voluntary trust.

The equitable remedy is employed to avoid unjust enrichment where the legal title to the property was obtained:

1) by fraud,

2) in violation of a fiduciary or confidential relationship,

3) by testamentary devise or intestate succession when the titleholder promised the testator that they would hold the property in trust for the benefit of someone else.

When a court finds that a constructive trust has been established, it will order the person whose conduct caused the constructive trustee to transfer title to and possession of the property held in the constructive trust to its rightful owner.

The circumstances which give rise to a constructive trust may be proven by oral evidence.

Neither the statute of frauds nor the parol evidence rule prevents a constructive trust from arising.

Fraud

If the property is conveyed to a person who makes a promise to use the property for a specific purpose and that person had no intent of fulfilling that promise when the property was conveyed, a court will impose a constructive trust upon the property requiring the grantee to use it for the intended purpose.

If the constructive trust remedy is not available because the grantor cannot prove an express trust and that the conveyance was procured by fraudulent intent, the grantor can recover the fair market value of the land based on a failure of consideration.

Violation of fiduciary or confidential relationship

A constructive trust will be imposed upon the property that is obtained in violation of a fiduciary relationship, such as attorney and client, trustee and beneficiary, physician and patient, business partners, employer and employee, corporate director or officer, and corporation or accountant and client.

Abuse of the fiduciary relationship can be shown by evidence of self-dealing or using confidential information to the advantage of the recipient at the expense of the one who disclosed the information or corporate opportunity.

Family relationship alone does not create fiduciary relationships but can be a factor if establishing one.

A fiduciary relationship does not ordinarily exist between businesspersons in arm's length relationships, but a confidential or fiduciary relationship may exist between those in a business relationship; if there is a misuse of confidential information.

Secret trusts on testamentary transfers

If a decedent fails to make a will and dies intestate, an express trust cannot be established.

If a decedent makes a will benefit an individual in reliance upon the oral promise of the person benefited by the will or by the intestacy that they use the inheritance to benefit another person, an express trust cannot be established.

A court can impose a constructive trust on the inheritance and require that the legatee use the property for fulfilling the promise made to the testator.

Relationship matrix

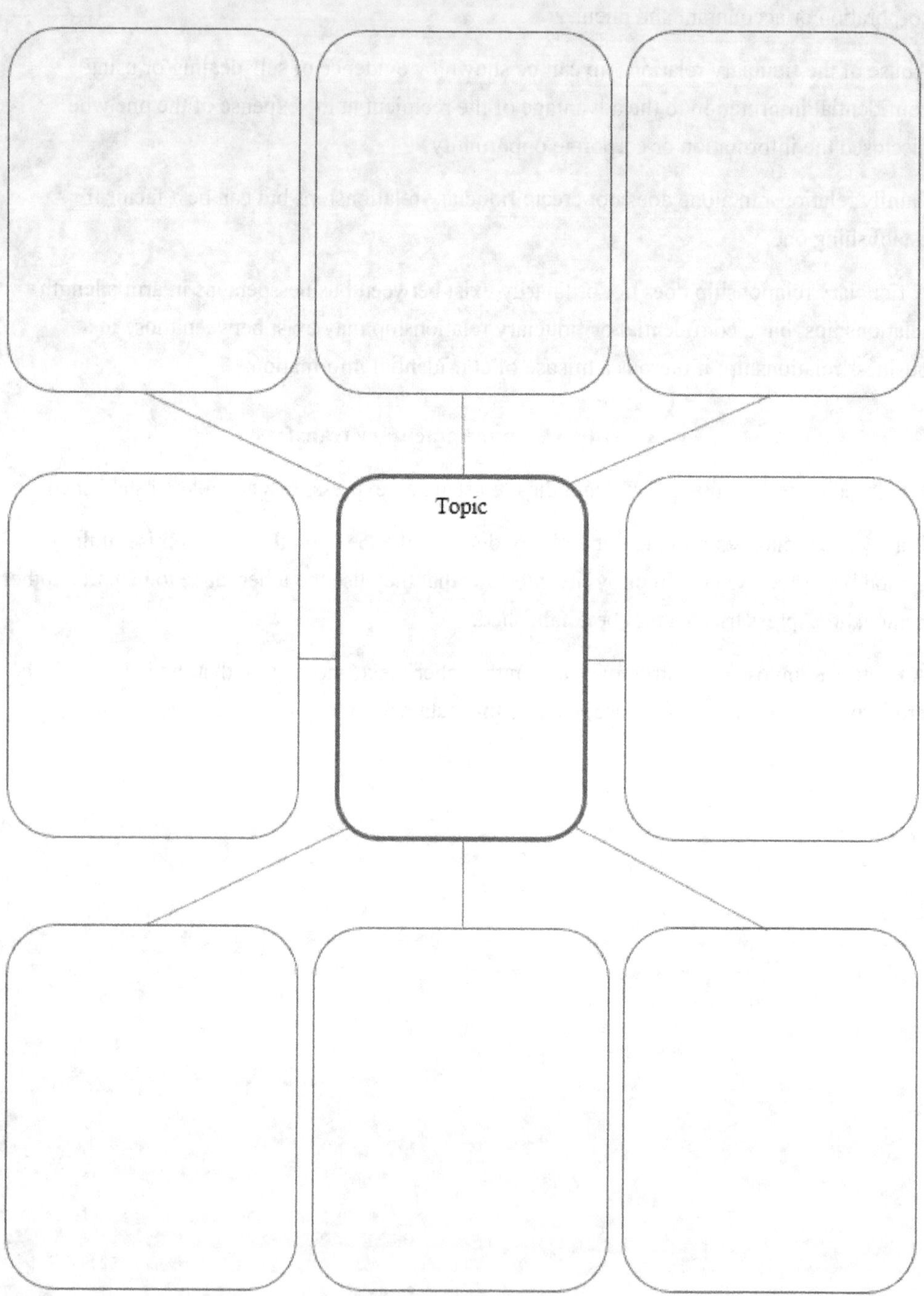

Notes for active learning

Notes for active learning

Review Questions

Multiple-choice questions

1. The type of trust created in a will is a:

   A. Testamentary trust   **C.** Implied trust

   B. *Inter vivos* trust   **D.** *Causa mortis* trust

2. The person who makes a will is the:

   I. Testator

   II. Testatrix

   III. Grantor

   A. I only   **C.** III only

   B. I and II only   **D.** I, II and III

3. The following methods can revoke at least part of a will:

   I. A subsequent will

   II. A divorce

   III. A codicil

   A. I only   **C.** I and III only

   B. I and II only   **D.** I, II and III

4. Testamentary capacity means that the person making the will must:

   A. Be of legal age and sound mind   **C.** Sign or initial every page

   B. Be witnessed before two witnesses   **D.** Have considerable assets

5. "To my beloved husband, I give you $500" is what type of gift?

   A. Residuary   **C.** Remainderman

   B. Specific   **D.** General

6. Intestate succession involves determining:

   A. Intestate property   **C.** Estate property

   B. Heirs   **D.** Escheat

7. Under the doctrine of ademption, the beneficiary:

    A. Is exempt from paying estate taxes
    B. Receives property remaining after taxes and creditors
    C. Renounces claim to inherited property
    D. Receives nothing

8. A will must, generally, be attested to by:

    A. The testator
    B. An attorney
    C. Competent witnesses
    D. Evidence of videotaping

9. A trust designed to prevent the beneficiary's creditors from getting the trust assets is a:

    A. Charitable trust
    B. Intestate trust
    C. Spendthrift trust
    D. Termination trust

10. If a testator leaves his red Ferrari to his former wife and the yellow Ferrari to his girlfriend, and at his death, the yellow Ferrari had been sold, which doctrine applies?

    A. Abatement
    B. Ademption
    C. Recidivism
    D. Bequestability

11. The legal way to make changes to an existing will is through a(n):

    A. Abatement
    B. Amendment
    C. Codicil
    D. Power of attorney

12. "If my niece has predeceased me, then I give my 1954 Aston Martin to my nephew" is what type of gift?

    A. Residuary
    B. Specific
    C. Bequestability
    D. General

13. A person on their deathbed may make the following type of will:

    I. Deathbed will
    II. Dying declaration will
    III. Nuncupative will

    A. I and III only
    B. II only
    C. III only
    D. I, II and III

14. A gift *causa mortis* is:

A. Made in contemplation of death **C.** Given during a person's lifetime

B. Dependent upon contract formation **D.** Irrevocable

15. When a testator distributes the same amount to all descendants, this method of gifting is:

A. Arbitrary and unfair **C.** *Per-stirpes*

B. Fair and equitable **D.** *Per-capita*

16. A residuary gift means:

A. A gift of the top twenty-five percent of the estate holdings

B. A portion of every gift distributed

C. A gift of anything left after other distributions

D. A gift of the homestead

17. The following is NOT required to make a will:

A. Testamentary capacity **C.** Self-proving clause

B. Writing **D.** Testator's signature

18. The elements that courts examine to determine undue influence include:

    I. The will contains a substantial benefit to the beneficiary

    II. The beneficiary assisted in the execution of the will

    III. The will has a distorted disposition of the testator's property

A. I only **C.** I and III only

B. I and II only **D.** I, II and III

True/false questions

19. A holographic will is captured in computer memory.

    True   False

20. The person who makes the will is the *testatum*.

    True   False

21. An *inter vivos* trust can be changed at the decision of the settlor.

    True   False

22. *"I hereby give to my administrative assistance my Cross pen"* is a specific gift.

    True   False

23. Generally, wills need not be in writing to be valid.

    True   False

24. Lineal descendants share equally without the degree of relationship for distribution *per stirpes*.

    True   False

25. A codicil must be executed in the same manner as a will.

    True   False

26. Gifts in a will can be specific, general, or residuary.

    True   False

27. Electronic recordings can supplement and strengthen a will.

    True   False

28. A holographic will must be in writing.

    True   False

29. A will may be revoked if the testator intentionally burns or tears the will.

    True   False

30. Attestation is when a will is adjudicated by a legal process to distribute property.

    True   False

31. Generally, an inheritance may not be renounced.

    True   False

32. A living will allows for the health care proxy to commit euthanasia.

    True   False

33. A nuncupative will must include the testator's signature.

    True   False

34. Most jurisdictions allow interested parties to act as witnesses to the will.

       True   False

Answer keys

1: A

2: B

3: D

4: A

5: D

6: B

7: C

8: C

9: C

10: B

11: C

12: A

13: D

14: A

15: D

16: C

17: C

18: D

19: False

20: False

21: True

22: True

23: False

24: False

25: True

26: True

27: True

28: True

29: True

30: False

31: False

32: False

33: False

34: False

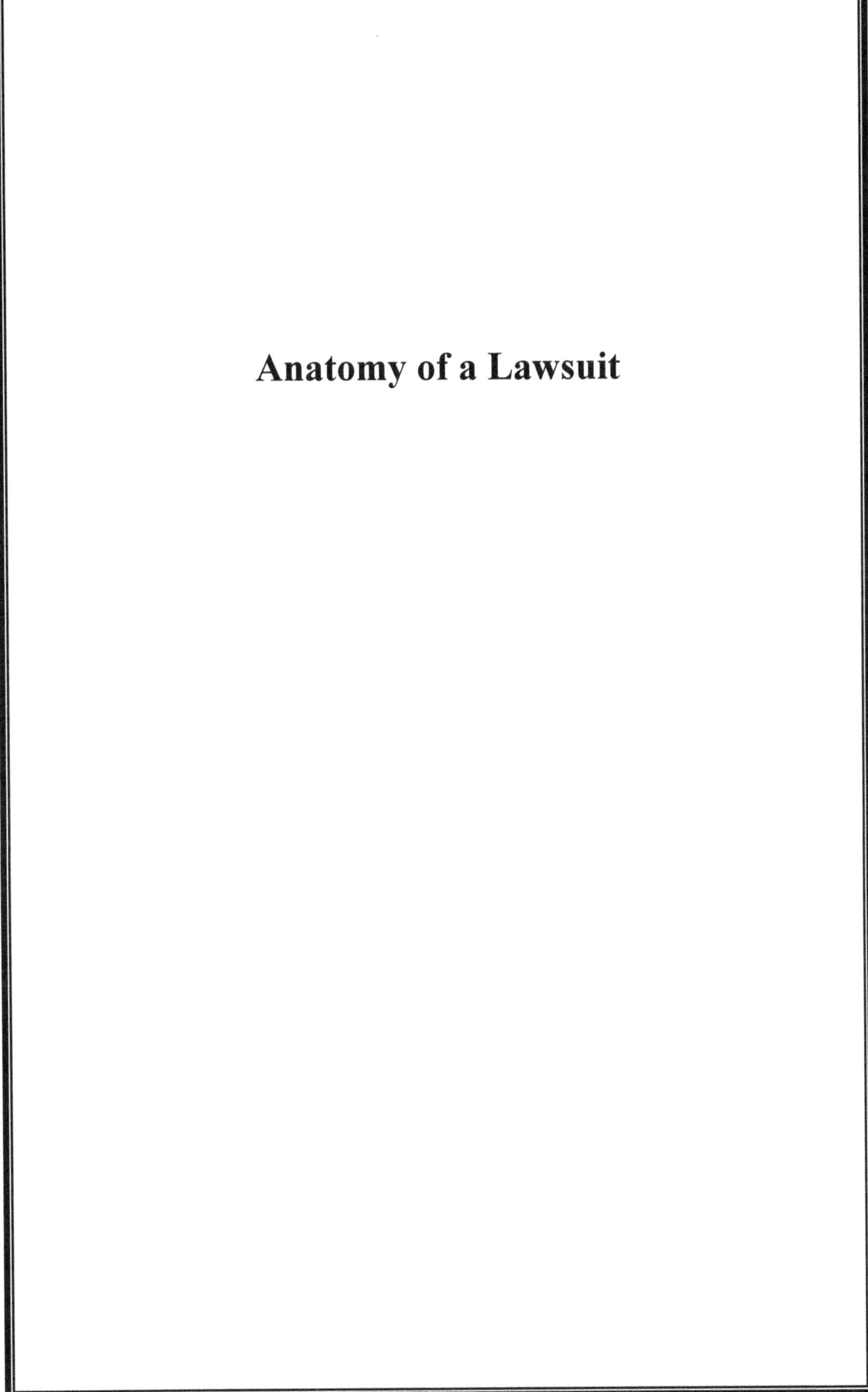

Anatomy of a Lawsuit

The Trial Process Overview

A lawsuit is a complicated legal process, whether suing, being sued, or acting as a witness. The legal process can have numerous unpleasant surprises and frustrating delays.

There are at least two parties to every action, and the court dictates the schedule and events. Some things happen in the same order in most litigation; the following chronology shows how a lawsuit proceeds. The actions may be different because of variations between state laws and rules of civil procedure.

At the start of a lawsuit, the legal papers filed in court are the pleadings (i.e., formal declarations of facts, claims, and the relief sought). Several documents become a part of a lawsuit, with some states have different names for the documents.

There are four main stages to a trial:

Pleading stage - filing the complaint and the defense's motions.

Pretrial stage - discovery process and finding of facts.

Trial stage - empaneling the jury, testimony on behalf of the plaintiffs, and testimony on behalf of the defendants.

Post-trial stage - concluding arguments, judge's charge to the jury, jury deliberations, announcement of judgment, motions for new trial or appeal.

Civil cases

A civil case begins when the plaintiff (i.e., person or entity) claims that the defendant (e.g., another person or entity) failed to perform a legal duty owed to the plaintiff. The plaintiff and the defendant are referred to as "parties" or "litigants." The plaintiff may ask the court to tell the defendant to fulfill the duty (i.e., performance) or make compensation (i.e., damages) for the harm done. Legal duties include respecting rights established under the Constitution, federal or state law.

For example, a lumberyard enters a contract to sell a specific amount of wood to a carpenter for an agreed-upon price. It fails to deliver the wood, forcing the carpenter to buy it elsewhere at a higher price. The carpenter might sue the lumberyard to pay the extra costs (i.e., damages) incurred because the lumberyard failed to deliver.

If these parties were from different states, that suit could be brought in federal court under diversity jurisdiction if the amount in question exceeded the minimum required by statute ($75,000.01).

Individuals, corporations, and the federal government can bring civil suits in federal court, claiming federal statutes or constitutional rights violations.

For example, the federal government can sue a hospital for overbilling Medicare and Medicaid, violating a federal statute. An individual could sue a local police department for violating their constitutional rights (e.g., the right to assemble peacefully).

Criminal cases

A person accused of a crime is generally charged in a formal accusation called an indictment (for felonies or serious crimes) or information (for misdemeanors). *On behalf of the people*, the government prosecutes the case through the United States Attorney's Office if the person is charged with a federal crime or the state's attorney's office (or district attorney) to prosecute state crimes.

It is not the victim's responsibility (nor right) to bring a criminal case. For example, the government would prosecute the kidnapper in a kidnapping case, and the victim would not be a party to the action. In some criminal cases, there may not be a specific victim. For example, state governments arrest and prosecute people accused of violating laws against driving while intoxicated because society regards that as a severe offense that can harm others.

When a court determines that an individual committed a crime, that person will receive a sentence. The sentence may be an order to pay a monetary penalty (e.g., restitution to the victim), imprisonment, supervision in the community, or some combination.

Intersection of civil and criminal cases

Civil cases involve disputes between (usually) private parties, while criminal cases are considered acts against the local or federal government. However, some acts may result in civil claims and criminal charges. For instance, a person may be sued for the intentional tort of assault or battery and may be arrested and charged with the crime of assault and battery.

There are times when a criminal act may give way to civil liability, such as when someone is charged with homicide and sued for wrongful death (typically follows the completion of the criminal trial). The criminal charges are punishable by fines, prison time, and other penalties, while the civil lawsuit focuses on recovering money to compensate the victim (or the victim's family) for damages.

Pleading Stage

The complaint initiates a lawsuit

A civil action (as opposed to a criminal or family proceeding, for example) begins with a *complaint*, usually accompanied by a *summons*. A complaint is a legal document that lays out the plaintiff's claims (the person bringing the lawsuit) has against the defendant (the person or business being sued).

The complaint (or *petition*) is the first document filed, which outlines the plaintiff's claims against the defendant. The complaint identifies the parties, sets the legal basis for the court's jurisdiction over the controversy, states the plaintiff's legal claims, relates the facts giving rise to the claims, and sets forth the plaintiff's request for relief. The plaintiff sets forth what they want the court to require the defendant to do, such as pay damages.

The complaint provides the defendant with notice of the factual and legal basis of the plaintiff's claims. Generally, the facts outlined in the complaint are based on the plaintiff's knowledge. The plaintiff may use the phrase "upon information and belief" for facts. The plaintiff may have learned about some facts from others and has formed a good-faith belief that the events are as described.

Most states require that the complaint set forth a *short and plain* statement of the plaintiff's claims. Often, the facts in the complaint are sparse and do not describe all events.

Summons

The summons is an order from the court where the lawsuit will be heard (i.e., litigated). The summons notifies the recipient (defendant) that they have been sued, refers to the complaint (or petition), and sets the time limit within which the defendant must file an answer or seek to have the case dismissed.

The summons describes the consequences of failing to respond promptly. For example, the case may be decided without the defendant, and the decision binds them. In jurisdictions where an action is commenced by service, the action can go on for a long time before the court ever becomes involved.

Failing to respond to a lawsuit on time causes the defendant to be *in default*.

Notice and service of process

The summons is delivered or *served* on the defendant along with the complaint. The summons is usually a form document with a preprinted caption that contains the name of the court, the parties, and a docket number (i.e., the court's identification number). The document informs the defendant that they have been sued; it serves as the *notice*.

Receipt is when somebody confirms their identity or mailed to the defendant; the *service of process.*

The summons, properly served, gives the court power (i.e., jurisdiction) over the dispute and the defendant. The court must have jurisdiction over the parties and issue described in the complaint. The decisions affecting the defendant are binding and enforceable for the litigated controversy.

Answer to the complaint

The defendant's response to the complaint is an *answer*, though some states use a different word. The answer addresses each paragraph in the complaint, and each response will ordinarily take one of three forms: "admitted," "denied," "insufficient knowledge to admit or deny." The answer says what portions of the complaint, if any, the defendant admits to, what the defendant contests, what defenses the defendant may have, and whether the defendant has claims against the plaintiff or others.

An answer may set forth various affirmative defenses, which are legal reasons why the defendant should not be held liable for the plaintiff's damages. Some of these defenses may be the basis of a motion to dismiss. The defendant must answer within a specific time (usually within weeks). If the defendant does not answer the complaint, the court may enter a default judgment.

Following the defendant's response to the plaintiffs' claims, the parties can choose to settle or request a judgment based on the evidence presented, or the court can decide to continue toward resolving the conflict at trial. If there is no judgment rendered, the case proceeds to the pretrial stage.

Counterclaim

If a defendant has a claim against the plaintiff, which arose out of the same circumstances as those that led to the complaint, it should be raised in the answer in a section entitled *counterclaims*. The counterclaim is written like the complaint.

If a defendant asserts a counterclaim in the answer, the plaintiff may respond by filing a *reply*. The reply admits, denies, or asserts that the plaintiff lacks information, just as the original answer did. The reply may assert defenses, just as the answer did.

Crossclaims

Crossclaims arise when two or more parties to the lawsuit, who are "aligned" as plaintiffs or defendants, have their dispute arising out of the same transaction or occurrence. A crossclaim is a claim against a party on the same side of an action.

Rule 13(g) of the Federal Rules of Civil Procedure, a crossclaim must be related to the original action in that it arises from the same transaction or occurrence as the original action or a counterclaim or involves property subject matter of the original action.

The person being sued in a crossclaim file an answer like the original complaint. For example, if Driver B and Driver C are sued by Driver A after a multiple-vehicle accident, and Driver C was injured by something Driver B did, Driver C might file a crossclaim against Driver B within the same lawsuit. The defendant will want to consider the various defenses available to them concerning the claim.

Third-party complaint

Sometimes a defendant who has been sued will have a legal reason for passing liability off to another person. This person may be brought into the lawsuit if the defendant files a third-party complaint. An example is a contract where the third party promises to pay another if the defendant is found liable.

The complaint sets forth the facts giving rise to the defendant's claim against the third party and requests relief. The party sued through a third-party complaint files an answer, similar to the one filed after the original complaint.

Notes for active learning

Discovery

A hallmark of the American legal system is the principle that there should be few surprises during a lawsuit. Since the late 1940s, the federal court system has required disclosing relevant facts and documents to the other side before trial, and virtually every state has followed this requirement. That disclosure is accomplished through a methodical process called *discovery*.

Discovery is the first phase in which the witness gets involved. Discovery takes three primary forms: written discovery (e.g., interrogatories) which must be answered under oath, document production, and depositions (i.e., sworn statements taken before a court officer). The parties exchange documents and other information about the litigation issues during discovery. The information is used in preparing the case for trial. Typically, third parties are involved in depositions, although there are provisions for written discovery and document requests to nonparties in many jurisdictions.

After discovery, the court typically reviews the facts of the case and determines if there is sufficient merit to proceed to trial or encourage the parties to settle. If the finding of facts determines the case to be frivolous or non-substantiated, the case is dismissed. If a substantial basis for the case is determined, the court will meet with and notify the parties of the trial schedule in the *pretrial order*.

Interrogatories and requests for admission

Interrogatories are questions requiring the opposing side's version of the facts and claims. They can be preprinted "form" interrogatories or specific questions asked. Questions can range from the broad ("What happened on Tuesday, June 18, 2021?") to the specific ("Is it your position that the defendant was wearing a blue jacket at 2:30 p.m. on May 13, 2021?"). If the questions asked are not fair or are difficult to understand, the party may object.

Requests for admission are not often used but can be a very powerful tool. They ask a party to admit or deny specific facts about the case, and they carry penalties for not answering, answering falsely, or answering late.

Document production

Each party has a right to see most documents arguably relate to a case. Particularly in more complex medical malpractice or product defect cases, the documents involved can be voluminous. Increasingly, courts are allowing access to computer files during document discovery. In cases where enough is at stake to justify it, courts have even allowed litigants to reconstruct deleted files (e.g., e-mail).

Depositions

Depositions are sworn statements when a person answers questions, and a court reporter makes a transcript of what is said. Depositions can range in length from an hour to weeks. Although attorneys have their strategies for depositions, there are three reasons to do them: to lock people into their stories, to see what the other side has, and to do a "practice trial," that is, to see how a witness will appear and conduct themselves before a judge or jury.

Depositions typically take place outside the courtroom, before a court recorder, with opposing counsel asking questions of the witness. The purpose of a deposition is to give facts, not speculate about what might have happened. Sometimes, "I don't know" is the correct answer. Second, it is human nature to want to explain things but resist the impulse. It is the opponent's responsibility to elicit the answers. The deponent should answer the question asked and not offer additional information.

Settlement avoids litigation

Most civil litigation cases never reach a final trial because a negotiated settlement is reached. Settlement ultimately means the plaintiff relinquishes their right to pursue the settled issue. For legal disputes, settlement can occur before or during litigation. Litigation is the dispute resolution process within the public court system after one party files a complaint and the other party answers. Settlement negotiation can be a formal or informal process. Parties can settle (i.e., agree) during informal negotiation or use a formal process called alternate dispute resolution (ADR), such as *mediation* or *arbitration*.

Some states and the federal system require litigants in civil actions to participate in alternative dispute resolution (ADR) in some form. The parties can agree to binding arbitration, and some contracts (insurance contracts and construction contracts, for example) require binding arbitration.

Often, the terms of the settlement are kept confidential. Sometimes, parties reach a settlement on specific issues in the case while a judge or jury needs to decide other issues. The Federal Rules of Evidence (and most state rules of evidence) provide that most settlement communications are inadmissible in court proceedings. Keeping these negotiations protected gives parties an incentive to have honest settlement discussions.

Typically, the court is either not involved or is involved informally. Judicial approval of civil settlements is usually required when one of the parties is a minor, a class action, or other circumstances that do not typically arise in most litigation.

Most criminal cases never go to trial either. Settlement may occur in criminal cases, though not in the same way as in civil cases. Sometimes, negotiations between the prosecution and defense lead to criminal charges being dismissed or a plea deal being reached. In criminal cases, the judge retains control over plea deals and can reject the agreement.

Motions to position the parties

In many cases, one or both parties try to have the dispute dismissed by motion. The parties present to the court those issues that are not in dispute, either because the parties agree or because the application of the law to the facts dictates a result.

The theory is that if a claim or lawsuit cannot possibly prevail, the parties and court should not waste time or money. Unfortunately, motion practice can be lengthy and expensive.

Summary judgment

In a trial, there are two overarching arguments. The attorneys argue about the law: determining which law applies and whether the law should be changed. Ultimately, questions of law are decided by the judge. The second argument is over the facts of each case, in other words, what happened. A jury usually decides the facts after considering testimony and other exhibits.

In many cases, the parties agree on some facts. When one party believes that there are no important facts in dispute, they file a motion for summary judgment. A typical summary judgment motion has three parts.

1) The facts: The plaintiff presents a version of the facts. The plaintiff usually attaches photos, signed statements from witnesses, and other evidence to support their statements.

2) The law: The plaintiff argues about the state of the law. The plaintiff's attorney prepares a memorandum that discusses the statutes and cases that govern the parties and attempt to convince the judge that, under the law, the plaintiff is entitled to win the case.

3) Even if…: In the last part of the summary judgment motion, the plaintiff anticipates what the defendant argues and tries to prove that the plaintiff will still win the case even if the defendant is correct in their arguments. For example, the plaintiff in a case about squatter's rights might claim they were living on a piece of property for 15 years but anticipates that the defendant will argue that the plaintiff has only been living on the property for 10 years. In this case, the plaintiff can argue that even if he had only been living on the property for 10 years, that is still enough time to win on a claim of squatter's rights.

The defendant responds. In their response, the defendant can show that the plaintiff's assertions about the law are incorrect, or evidence supports more than one version of the facts.

The judge's decision. After the papers and supporting evidence have been submitted, the judge reviews the paperwork and decides. The judge will grant the motion or agree with (in this example) the plaintiff if:

1) the plaintiff's arguments about the law were correct, and

2) even assuming the defendant's version of the facts was true, the plaintiff wins.

The judge will deny the motion if there is evidence that presents facts at trial.

Change of venue

Two basic requirements must be met before a court can hear a case.

1) *jurisdiction*, which means that the court can decide the legal issues affecting the parties' rights.

2) *venue*, which decides whether the court is in the best location to hear the case. Although this may sound unimportant, there are strict rules concerning where a case may be heard.

When one party wants to change venue, they must file a motion for change of venue. A motion for a change of venue ensures that a case is heard in the best location.

Most jurisdictions have strict requirements for the motion, which can be found in that jurisdiction's rules of procedure. Usually, a memorandum of law must accompany this motion, laying out the law and the arguments for why the venue should be moved. There are famous (or infamous) cases in a locality, and a party may wish to change venue so that jurors are less likely to have heard of the case and, therefore, be unbiased. Each state and federal jurisdiction has rules concerning venue

There are often rules about when a motion for change of venue may be filed during a case. If the venue is not challenged at the proper time, a challenge may be precluded.

Statutes of limitations

There are definite time limits to file a lawsuit. It depends upon the state (or federal law) and the offense. Some claims expire within a year after the event. Other claims can be filed decades later (e.g., tax fraud).

There are several ways that a statute of limitation may start, but the common three are:

1) The "date of harm." For example, the day you have a traffic accident will typically start the statute of limitations for suits regarding property damage to your car.

2) The date the harm was first discovered. The harm may lie dormant for a while and be discovered later. For example, hidden property damage until an inspection.

3) The date the harm should have been discovered. This is a less common standard, but in some instances, the period starts when the plaintiff should have discovered the harm, not when they did.

An exception is if the plaintiff sues a government agency. Because the government writes the rules, they have made it particularly difficult to sue them. In some instances, as little as 60 days to file a lawsuit is required to file an administrative complaint before filing a lawsuit.

There is much variation depending on the claim. Some statutes of limitations are:

- Libel or slander – 1 year

- Personal injury – 2 years

- Domestic violence – 3 years

- Medical malpractice – 3 years

- Breach of written contract – 4 years

- Breach of oral contract – 2 years

Notes for active learning

Trial Stage

The trial

If the parties do not reach an agreement or the dispute is not disposed of by motion, the case goes to trial. A trial is the plaintiff's opportunity to argue their case for obtaining a judgment against the defendant. A trial represents the defendant's chance to refute the plaintiff's case and offer evidence related to the dispute. In a civil trial, a judge or jury examines the evidence to decide whether, by a "preponderance of the evidence," the defendant should be held legally responsible for the damages alleged by the plaintiff.

Although a trial is the most high-profile phase of a civil lawsuit, most civil disputes are resolved before trial (or before a lawsuit is filed) via settlement between the parties. This process can include alternative dispute resolution (ADR) like arbitration or dismissal of the case.

The following six main phases of a civil trial is presented in the context of a typical "plaintiff *v.* defendant civil case.

1) Jury selection

2) Opening statements

3) Witness testimony and cross-examination

4) Closing arguments

5) Jury instructions

6) Jury deliberation and verdict

At trial, the attorneys (or the parties, if they are not represented) present evidence and legal arguments, and the judge (or jury) decides the facts. The trial is the other point at which third parties can become involved. The attorney for the party who wants a person to testify may subpoena them for trial. Witnesses can be called to testify at any time, from shortly after the event to almost a decade after.

After both sides present their arguments, the judge or jury considers whether to find the defendant liable for the plaintiff's claimed damages, and if so, to what extent (i.e., the amount of money damages a defendant must pay, or fashion another remedy).

Depending on the type of case, a civil trial may not necessarily focus only on the plaintiff's allegations and the defendant's liability. For example, in most divorce cases, a trial judge decides after hearing allegations from both sides of the dispute and enters a judgment that may favor one spouse on one issue (e.g., child custody) and the other spouse as to another issue (e.g., alimony). Once the judge or jury has reached a decision, the judge orders judgment. The judge may order that one party pay the attorney's fees, although such awards are unusual.

Either party may appeal a judge's decision to a higher court. However, it is unusual for an appeals court to overturn a judge's decision. Settlements usually cannot be appealed if both parties agree to their terms. The process can take from six months to years. Generally, the less money in dispute and the more issues are resolved before trial, the faster the lawsuit.

Jury selection

In most civil cases, either party can choose to have a jury. Whether to request a jury is extremely important. Except in cases that are tried before a judge (e.g., family court cases), an initial step in a civil trial is selecting a jury.

During jury selection, the judge (and usually the attorneys) questions a pool of potential jurors regarding general matters or about knowledge or preformed opinions about the case – this process is *voire dire*. These questions probe personal ideological predispositions or life experiences that pertain to the case. The judge can excuse potential jurors at this stage based on their responses.

Either the plaintiff or defendant may exclude a certain number of jurors by using peremptory challenges and challenges for cause.

A *peremptory challenge* excludes a juror for any reason.

A *challenge for cause* excludes a juror who cannot be objective in deciding the case.

Opening statements

Once a jury is selected, the first "dialogue" in a personal injury trial comes in the form of two opening statements -- one from the plaintiff's attorney and the other from an attorney representing the defendant.

Statements to the jury made first by the plaintiffs' attorney and then by the defense attorneys setting up the circumstances and rationale of the legal complaint (plaintiffs) and the reasons for dismissing the claim (defense). No witnesses testify at this stage, and no physical evidence is ordinarily utilized.

Because the plaintiff must demonstrate the defendant's legal liability based on the plaintiff's allegations, the plaintiff's opening statement is usually given first. It is often more detailed than that of the defendant. In some cases, the defendant may wait until the plaintiff's main case concludes before making its opening statement.

Regardless of when opening statements are made in a personal injury case, during those statements:

- The plaintiff presents the facts of the case and the defendant's alleged role in causing the plaintiff's damages (or reasons to find for the plaintiff) -- walking the jury through what the plaintiff intends to demonstrate to get a civil judgment against the defendant.

- The defendant's attorney gives the jury the defense's interpretation of the facts and sets the stage for rebutting the plaintiff's key evidence and presenting any "affirmative" defenses to the plaintiff's allegations (or reasons to find for the defendant).

When a civil lawsuit involves multiple parties (i.e., three individual plaintiffs sue one defendant, or one plaintiff sues two separate defendants), attorneys representing each party may give distinct opening arguments.

Evidence and arguments

Plaintiff testimony

At the heart of any civil trial is often called the "case-in-chief," the stage at which each side presents its key evidence and arguments to the jury. In its case-in-chief, the plaintiff methodically sets forth its evidence to convince the jury that the defendant is legally responsible for the plaintiff's damages or that judgment for the plaintiff is warranted under the circumstances.

At this point, the plaintiff may call witnesses and experts to testify to strengthen their case. The plaintiff may introduce physical evidence, such as photographs, documents, and medical reports.

In complicated civil lawsuits (e.g., employment discrimination, defective product claims), plaintiffs use expert testimony and documentary evidence as crucial in proving the defendant's legal liability. Documents must be authentic. There are many evidence rules to ensure that the item in evidence is the actual evidence, or at least an accurate copy. The rules of evidence govern what may and may not be considered when the jury decides the outcome of a case.

Defense testimony

After the plaintiff concludes its case-in-chief and "rests," the defendant can present its evidence in the same proactive manner, seeking to show that it is not liable for the plaintiff's claimed harm. The defense may call its witnesses to the stand and present independent evidence to refute or downplay the key elements of the plaintiff's allegations.

Once the defense has rested, the plaintiff has an opportunity to respond to the defense's arguments through a process known as "rebuttal," a brief period during which the plaintiff may only contradict the defense's evidence (rather than present new arguments). Sometimes, the defense may, in turn, have a chance to respond to the prosecution's rebuttal.

Once the plaintiff and defendant each present their case and challenge the evidence presented by the other, both sides "rest," meaning that no more evidence will be presented to the jury before closing arguments are made.

Witness testimony and cross-examination

Whether called by the plaintiff or defendant, witness testimony usually adheres to the following formula:

- The witness is called to the stand and is "sworn in," taking an oath *to tell the truth.*

- The party who called the witness to the stand questions the witness through "direct" examination, eliciting information through question-and-answer to strengthen the party's position in the dispute.

- After direct examination, the opposing party has an opportunity to question the witness through "cross-examination." Cross-examination tries to discredit the witness's story, credibility, or otherwise discredit the witness and their testimony.

- After cross-examination, the side that originally called the witness has a second opportunity to question him or her through "re-direct examination" and attempt to remedy any damaging effects of cross-examination.

Witnesses may only present facts that they observed. A witness can say, "I saw the blue car drive through a red light before hitting the pedestrian," but a witness cannot say something like, "The driver of the blue car should go to jail because he ran a red light and hurt someone," because it is the witness's opinion that the driver should go to jail. Lawyers are not allowed to ask leading questions, such as "Where did the blue car go through the red light?" because it suggests to the witness that this event occurred.

Every witness must be able to be cross-examined. Cross-examination is the part of the trial when one attorney tries to discover untruths or other issues with a witness's testimony. The right to cross-examine stems from the 6th Amendment right of the accused to confront the accuser. It ensures that all testimony is rigorously examined before going to a jury. "Hearsay testimony" are statements about what another told the witness and are generally not allowed when the original person is not in court. However, there are exceptions to this rule.

At the discretion of the judge, each witness can be redirected after cross-examination by either counsel. If critical information is not divulged during the initial testimony, counsel can request to *recall* a witness to the stand for additional questioning and cross-examination.

Judges rule on objections

When a lawyer says "objection" during court, they tell the judge that they think their opponent violated a rule of procedure. The judge's ruling determines what the jury is allowed to consider when deciding the verdict of a case.

A judge can either "overrule" the objection or "sustain" it. When an objection is overruled, it means that the evidence is properly admitted to the court, and the trial can proceed.

When an objection is sustained, the lawyer must rephrase the question or otherwise address the issue with the evidence to ensure that the jury only hears properly admitted evidence. In theory, the jury should disregard the improper question asked, although this can be difficult to do.

An objection is essential to procedure even if it is overruled. Once a lawyer objects to some evidence, that objection is on the record. If the lawyer disagrees with the judge's ruling, they can appeal that decision. If the lawyer failed to object to evidence, they lose the right to appeal, even if the evidence was admitted improperly.

Closing arguments

Like the opening statement, the closing argument offers the plaintiff and the defendant in a civil dispute a chance to "sum up" the case, recapping the evidence in a light favorable to their respective positions. This is the final chance for the parties to address the jury before deliberations.

In closing arguments, the plaintiff seeks to show why the evidence requires the jury to find the defendant legally responsible for the plaintiff's damages or why the plaintiff's case is stronger than the defendants. The defendant tries to show that the plaintiff has fallen short of establishing the defendant's liability for any civil judgment in the plaintiff's favor.

Closing arguments are typically intended to be dramatic and pointed for effect.

Jury instruction

After both sides have presented their arguments and evidence, the judge (in a bench trial) or jury (jury trial) considers whether to find the defendant liable for the plaintiff's damages, and if so, to what extent (i.e., the amount of money damages a defendant must pay, or some other remedy).

Jury instructions are the process in which the judge gives the jury the set of legal standards needed to decide whether the defendant should be held accountable for the plaintiff's alleged harm.

The judge decides what legal standards apply to the defendant's case based on the issues and evidence presented during the trial. Often, this process has input from the plaintiff and defendant. The judge instructs the jury on relevant legal principles, including findings the jury must make to arrive at certain conclusions. The judge describes critical legal concepts (e.g., "preponderance of the evidence"), defines claims the jury may consider (i.e., *fraud, breach of contract, emotional distress*); and discusses types of damages (i.e., compensatory, and punitive) based on the evidence presented at trial.

After the judge provides the jury with specific oral instructions regarding its evaluation of the case, the jury is dismissed to deliberate, in private, the outcome of the case.

Jury deliberation, verdict and judgment

After receiving instruction from the judge, the jurors as a group consider the case through a process of "deliberation" and attempt to agree on whether the defendant should be held liable based on the plaintiff's claims. If so, the appropriate compensation for any damages. Deliberation is the first opportunity for the jury to discuss the case. Deliberations are a methodical process lasting from a few hours to several weeks.

Once the jury reaches a decision (may take hours to days), the jury foreperson informs the judge, and the judge announces the verdict in open court.

Most states require that a 12-person jury in a personal injury case be unanimous in finding for the plaintiff or the defendant, though some states allow for verdicts based on a majority as low as 9 to 3.

If the jury fails to reach a unanimous (or sufficient majority) verdict and is at a standstill (i.e., a *hung* jury), the judge may declare a *mistrial*; the case may be dismissed, or a trial starts again with jury selection.

Following the rendering of the verdict, the court can rule and concur requesting final judgment or determine if a new trial is required or if the case should be dismissed.

Post-Trial Stage

Appealing a court decision

Most civil and criminal decisions of a state or federal trial court (and administrative decisions by agencies) are subject to review by an appeals court. Whether the appeal concerns a judge's order or a jury's verdict, an appeals court reviews what happened in prior proceedings for any errors of law or procedure. The losing party cannot appeal a case just because they are unhappy with the outcome; they may only challenge decisions that may have resulted from errors, such as a misinterpretation of legal precedent or reliance on evidence that should have been excluded and not presented to the jury.

If the court finds an error contributing to the trial court's decision, the appeals court will reverse that decision. The parties submit briefs to the court and may be granted an oral argument before the panel of judges. Once an appeals court has made its decision, the opportunity for further appeals is limited. As the number of parties filing appeals has risen substantially, the state and federal court systems have implemented changes to manage the appeals process.

Trials *vs.* appeals

A trial and an appeal have a few similarities but many significant differences. The parties present their cases at trial, call witnesses for testimony, and present evidence (e.g., documents, photographs, reports, surveys, diaries). The jury evaluates the veracity of the evidence and determines the facts of the case; what they believe happened. A jury is sometimes referred to as the "finder of fact."

The judge controls the activities in the courtroom and makes the legal decisions, such as ruling on motions and objections raised by the attorneys. The judge is often called the "finder of law." If the parties have chosen a bench trial rather than a jury trial, the judge makes both fact and law findings.

Appeals overview

An appeal is a review of the trial court's application of the law. There is no jury in an appeal, nor do the lawyers present witnesses or other evidence. The court accepts the facts as revealed in the trial court unless a factual finding is clearly against the weight of the evidence.

Another difference between a trial and an appeal is the number of judges involved. A single judge presides over a trial while several judges hear an appeal, depending on the jurisdiction. At the initial appeals court level, courts may have three to a few dozen (en banc) judges.

However, the total number of judges seldom hear claims together. Instead, appeals are typically heard by panels, often comprised of three judges. In rare instances, the full court may decide to grant a motion for rehearing *en banc* when all the judges on the appeals court hear the case and issue a decision. At the state and federal level, Supreme Courts have from five to nine justices (i.e., justices are judges on the highest appeals court in the jurisdiction).

Appellate briefs

The main form of persuasion on appeal is the written appellate brief, filed by counsel for each party. With this brief, the party that lost in the trial court argues that the trial judge incorrectly applied the law. The party that won below will argue that the trial court's decision was correct. Both parties support their positions concerning applicable case law and statutes.

An appeal is a more scholarly proceeding than a trial. Whereas the litigator must be an active strategist in the courtroom, calling witnesses, cross-examining, and making motions or objections, the appellate lawyer builds their case in the brief before the appeal is heard. Appeals often include a short period for oral argument, but the judges often consume this period with questions for the attorney, prompted by the briefs.

The "record" on appeal

Appeals court decisions turn on the record, which documents what happened in the trial court. The record contains the pleadings (i.e., plaintiff's complaint and defendant's answer), pretrial motions, a transcript of what occurred during the trial, the exhibits put into evidence, post-trial motions, and any discussion with the judge that did not take place "off the record." The success of an appeal, therefore, depends on what occurred at trial. If an attorney fails to get critical, available evidence into the record or object to something prejudicial, the opportunity to do so is lost.

Post appeal

The party that loses in a state or federal appeals court may appeal to the state supreme court or the U.S. Supreme Court. Most states call their highest court *Supreme Court*, though Maryland and New York call theirs the *Court of Appeals*.

Review in appeals courts, however, is discretionary. Because the U.S. Supreme Court receives many more requests for review than practical, they typically grant review only to cases involving unsettled questions of law (e.g., different decisions within the federal circuit courts). The U.S. Supreme Court can only review cases that raise federal or constitutional issues. Cases concerning state law exclusively are beyond Supreme Court jurisdiction. At the highest appellate court, the parties have litigated and had the case reviewed at least once, reducing decisions that are biased or contrary to law.

Notes for active learning

Civil Litigation Timeline

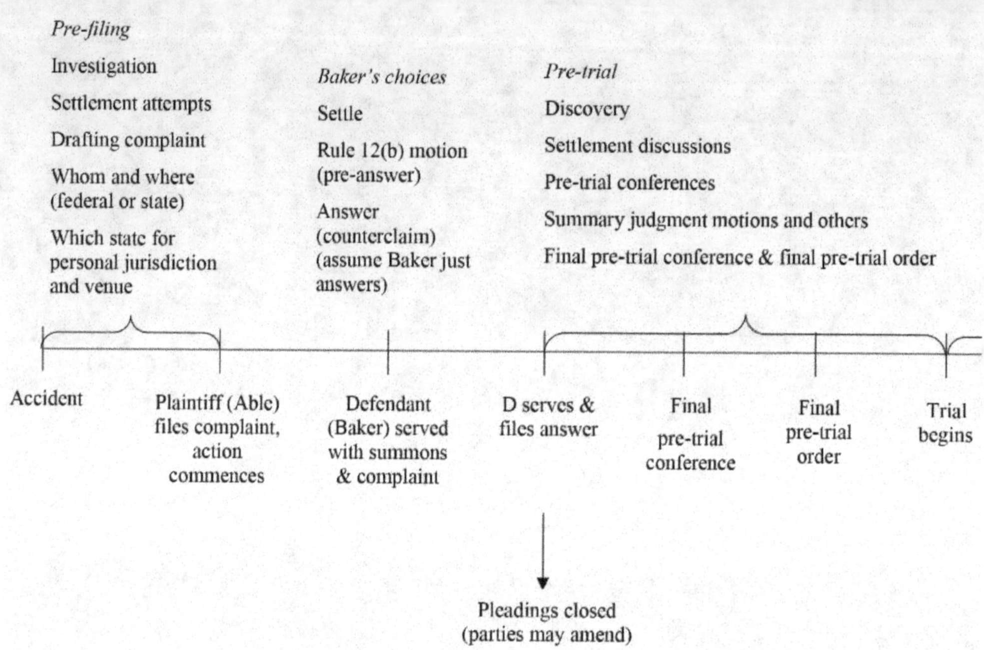

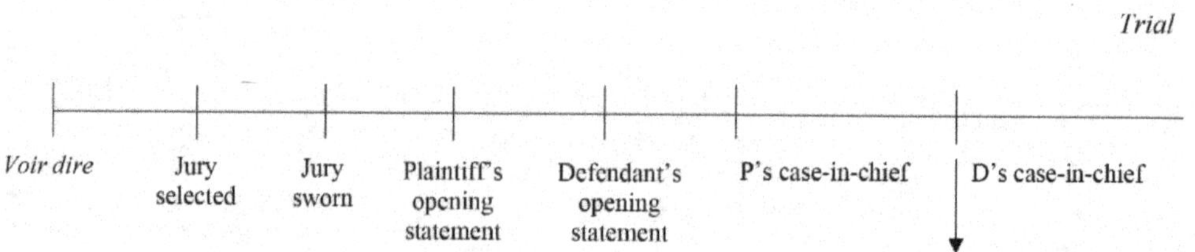

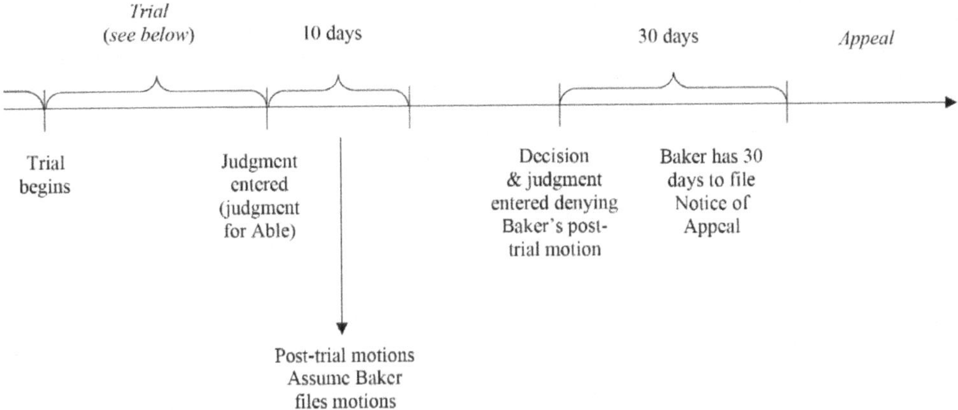

Trial
(see below)
10 days
30 days
Appeal
Trial
begins
Judgment
entered
(judgment
for Able)
Decision
& judgment
entered denying
Baker's post-
trial motion
Baker has 30
days to file
Notice of
Appeal
Post-trial motions
Assume Baker
files motions

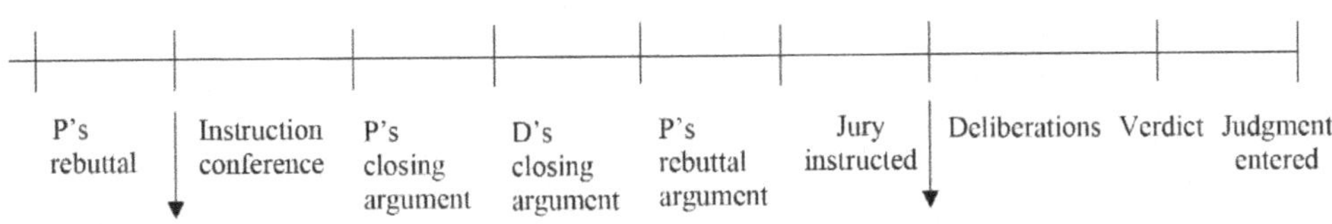

P's
rebuttal
Instruction
conference
P's
closing
argument
D's
closing
argument
P's
rebuttal
argument
Jury
instructed
Deliberations
Verdict
Judgment
entered

Notes for active learning

Subpoenas

A *subpoena* [Latin, *under penalty*] is a court-ordered command to produce documents or appear for a proceeding.

The subpoena requires a person to *do* something (e.g., testify, present information) as facts in a pending case.

A *subpoena ad testificandum* requires a person to testify before a court or other legal authority.

A *subpoena duces tecum* requires a person to produce documents, materials, or tangible evidence.

A subpoena may be requested in any matter, but common issues involve divorce, child custody, and personal injury.

Purpose of a subpoena

Under state and federal civil procedure, subpoenas offer parties a chance to obtain information to prove their case.

Criminal attorneys use subpoenas to obtain *witness* or *lay opinion* (i.e., personal experience) testimony from a third party to support the defendant's innocence.

Civil attorneys subpoena individuals and businesses for information that may help settle a claim.

For example, an attorney representing a spouse in a child custody hearing might issue a subpoena to the other spouse to appear in court to determine joint custody arrangements.

Examples of subpoenas include requests for computer files and downloaded material, income tax returns, photographs, graphs, & charts, blood test results, DNA samples, medical, insurance, and employee records.

Authority to issue subpoenas

A subpoena is typically requested by an attorney and issued by a court clerk, magistrate, or judge.

For specific purposes, a subpoena may be issued and signed by an attorney on behalf of the court in which the attorney is authorized to practice law.

If the subpoena is for a high-level government official (e.g., governor, agency head), it must be signed by an administrative law judge.

In some cases, a non-lawyer may issue a subpoena if acting on their behalf (*pro se* litigant).

Serving a subpoena

Depending on the jurisdiction, a subpoena may be served as follows:

> Hand-delivered (known as "personal delivery" method);

> E-mailed to the last known e-mail address of the individual (receipt acknowledgment requested);

> Certified mail to the last known address (return receipt requested); or

> Hearing it read aloud.

Responding to a subpoena

A subpoena is part of a court's legal process, and failure to respond is considered *contempt of court*.

The subpoena specifies what is requested or who is to appear.

Subpoena requests for documents are detailed, allowing adequate preparation for testimony at trial or proceeding.

Penalties for failure to comply

A subpoena is a court-ordered command. A person who receives a subpoena but does not comply with its terms may be subject to civil or criminal contempt of court charges and penalties (e.g., fines, jail time, or both).

Civil contempt occurs when a person fails to produce documents requested or fails to obey the terms of a subpoena and, thereby, hinders the judicial process.

Penalties for contempt of court include fines, imprisonment, or both.

Contempt charges apply until the party agrees to produce the requested information and perform legal obligations.

Criminal contempt, usually intended as punishment, refers to disruptive conduct or disrespectful behavior at court.

Criminal contempt includes the refusal to submit documents or other data.

Refusing to produce documents

Defenses for failure to produce documents or appear in court may include claims that the information sought is privileged, lost, violates a person's Fifth Amendment right against self-incrimination, or the requests are overbroad or unduly burdensome.

Alternative Dispute Resolution (ADR)

Alternative dispute resolution (ADR) advantages and disadvantages

Using the court system to resolve disputes can take years and cost thousands, if not millions, for legal fees and expenses. Parties increasingly use alternative dispute resolution (ADR) methods to resolve disputes. The advantages of ADR, as compared to traditional litigation, are the efficiency of costs and time. ADR saves much money, in large part because it saves much time. In commercial litigation, the ordinary business operations of the parties are often disrupted. Moreover, because ADR is faster and less expensive than traditional litigation, it is much less stressful for the participants, which is another advantage.

There are some disadvantages of ADR, however. The process has been criticized as a waste of time by some legal commentators who believe that the same time could be spent pursuing civil court claims. ADR prevents the parties from getting their day in court, and for some litigants, this is a reason to use adversarial litigation. Arbitration awards, for instance, are challenging to overturn on appeal.

Types of ADR

Several processes qualify as *alternative dispute resolution* (ADR). Parties may agree that a negotiated settlement is preferred to investing time and money in protracted civil litigation.

Common forms of ADR include negotiation, mediation, arbitration, conciliation, minitrials, and fact-finding.

Many ADR techniques have little in common except that negotiation is prominent. Mediation and arbitration and are frequently used alternative dispute resolution techniques.

Negotiation

Negotiation plays a vital role in each method, either primarily or secondarily. For example, it is not uncommon for parties to begin negotiations with early neutral evaluation and then move to nonbinding mediation. If mediation fails, the parties may proceed with binding arbitration. The goal with each type of ADR is for the parties to find the most effective way of resolving their dispute without litigation. Many participants in unsuccessful ADR proceedings believe it is helpful to determine that their disputes are not amenable to a negotiated settlement before commencing a lawsuit.

Conciliation

Conciliation focuses on the early stages of negotiation, such as opening communication channels, bringing the disputants together, and identifying points of mutual agreement. Mediation focuses on the later stages of negotiation, exploring weaknesses in each party's position, investigating areas where the parties disagree but might be inclined to compromise, and suggesting mutually agreeable outcomes.

Mediation

Mediation consists of assisted negotiations where the disputants agree to enlist a neutral intermediary. The mediator facilitates a voluntary, mutually acceptable settlement. Their primary function is to identify issues, explore agreements, discuss the consequences of an impasse, and encourage considering the other party's interests. However, unlike arbitrators, mediators lack the power to impose a decision on the parties.

Mediation is referred to as conciliation or conciliated negotiation. However, the terms are not necessarily interchangeable. Conciliation and mediation typically work well when the disputants are involved in a long-term relationship (e.g., married partners, wholesalers, retailers) and intricate problems not easily solved by all-or-nothing solutions (e.g., antitrust suits with many complex issues).

Although some jurisdictions have enacted statutes governing mediation, most mediation proceedings are voluntary. Accordingly, a mediator's influence is limited by the autonomy of the parties and their willingness to negotiate in good faith. Thus, a mediator can go no further than the parties are willing to go.

Since agreements reached by mediation bear the parties' imprint, many observers feel more likely to adhere to decisions imposed than arbitration or court mandates. Disputants who participate in mediation without legal representation are likely to adhere to settlements when the alternative is civil litigation. Attorneys' fees consume a significant portion of any monetary award granted to the parties.

Arbitration

Arbitration refers the dispute to an impartial intermediary chosen by the parties who agree to abide by the arbitrator's award issued after a hearing where the parties have the opportunity to be heard. Arbitration resembles traditional civil litigation in that a neutral intermediary hears arguments and imposes a final and binding decision.

In arbitration, the parties elect to settle future disputes without judicial intervention. The disputants select the intermediary who serves as an arbitrator. Arbitration resembles litigation as parties use arbitration for facilitated settlement negotiations. Parties using arbitration often fail to commence serious negotiations until the arbitration proceedings begin.

In civil litigation, the judicial system is generally chosen by an aggrieved party after a dispute has materialized. Thus, parties to civil litigation have little to no control over who presided in the judicial proceedings.

Frequently, negotiations continue with the arbitration proceedings, the parties' representatives discuss settlement as hearings are underway. Arbitration expedites negotiations since the parties know that the decision is typically final and rarely appealable once the arbitrator issues a decision.

Private arbitration

Private contractual arbitration agreements are used by parties where disputes arise and prefer alternative dispute resolutions compared to a judicial remedy. The arbitrator need not be a judge or government official. Instead, an effective arbitrator is a person whom the parties feel has knowledge, experience, and objectivity to resolve the dispute. In some states, legislation prescribes the qualifications to be an arbitrator.

An arbitrator's power is derived from the arbitration agreement, limiting issues that the arbitrator has the authority to resolve. In many states, arbitration agreements are supported by statutes providing judicial enforcement of agreements and respecting arbitrator-rendered awards.

Statutes governing private arbitration often set forth criteria that must be followed before an arbitration agreement is binding and enforceable by a court. A court typically deems the arbitrator's decision final, and the losing party may only appeal the decision upon a showing of fraud, misrepresentation, or arbitrariness by the arbitrator.

Private arbitration is the primary method of settling labor disputes between unions and employers. For example, unions and employers include a collective bargaining arbitration agreements clause in contracts. The union and employer agree to arbitrate future employee grievances (e.g., wages, hours, working conditions, job security). Many real estate and insurance contracts specify arbitration as the exclusive resolution method for disputes between the parties entering into these types of relationships.

Judicial arbitration

Judicial arbitration is a non-binding form of arbitration. Judicial arbitration is usually mandated by statute or court rules that govern disputes exceeding the jurisdiction of small claims court but insufficient for trial in civil court. A party dissatisfied with the arbitrator's decision may proceed to trial rather than accept the decision. Most jurisdictions prescribe a specific period within which the parties to a judicial arbitration may reject the arbitrator's decision and litigate. If this period expires before either party rejects the arbitrator's decision, the decision becomes final, binding, and judicially enforceable, like a private arbitrator's decision.

Non-binding judicial arbitration in federal court

Several federal district courts also have mandatory programs for non-binding judicial arbitration funded by Congress. For example, the Local Rules of Court may require non-binding arbitration for disputes not expected to exceed $200,000. Since judicial arbitration is mandatory but non-binding, it facilitates settlement negotiations. Arbitration reduces civil court calendars that may have hundreds of lawsuits to improve judicial efficiency.

The policy is that by mandating nonbinding arbitration, the parties value a negotiated settlement. Seldom do litigants receive everything demanded in their petitions or complaints. Private and judicial arbitration is generally less costly and more time-efficient than formal civil litigation. The typical arbitration takes 4 to 5 months, while litigation may take years. The cost of arbitration is minimal compared to civil trials since the American Arbitration Association charges a nominal filing fee. The arbitrator may work without a fee to broaden their professional experience.

Minitrials

A minitrial is a process by which the attorneys present a brief version of the case to a panel, often comprised of the clients and a neutral intermediary who chairs the process. Expert witnesses (or lay witnesses) present the case. After the presentation, the clients, typically top management representatives, attempt to negotiate a settlement. If a negotiated settlement is not reached, the parties may allow the intermediary to mediate the dispute or render a non-binding advisory opinion regarding the likely outcome if tried in civil court.

Businesses use minitrials to resolve large-scale disputes involving product liability, antitrust issues, billion-dollar construction contracts, and mass tort or disaster litigation. Minitrials are effective because they bring top management together to negotiate the legal issues underlying a dispute. Early in the negotiation process, upper management is sometimes preoccupied with the business side of a dispute. Minitrials shift management's focus to outstanding legal issues. Minitrials allow businesses a forum for face-to-face negotiations. Management also generally prefers the time-saving, abbreviated nature of minitrials over time-consuming and costly civil litigation. Minitrials expedite negotiations by making them more realistic. Once the parties have seen their case play out in court, they are less likely to posture over less relevant or meaningless issues.

Summary jury trials

Summary jury trials are used primarily in federal courts. They allow parties to *litigate* their cases before an advisory panel of jurors without a final decision as rendered by a jury in civil court. The purpose of the summary jury trial is to facilitate pretrial settlement. A significant impediment to negotiation is a disagreement between the parties (and their attorneys) regarding a civil jury's likely findings on liability or damages. Like minitrials, summary jury trials give the parties a chance to reach a preliminary assessment of the strengths and weaknesses and proceed with negotiations after the advisory jury's findings.

Summary jury trials and minitrials can be scheduled and completed before formal civil cases usually reach the court docket. Summary jury trials are presided over by a judge or magistrate in a federal district court. Evidentiary and procedural rules are few and flexible. For example, a ten-member jury venire is presented to counsel. Counsel is provided with a short juror character profile and given two challenges to select a final six-member jury for the proceeding. Each attorney has one hour to argue their case to the jury.

After counsel's presentations, the presiding official delivers a brief statement of the applicable law to the jury, and the jury retires to deliberate. Juries are encouraged to return a consensus verdict but may return a special report that anonymously lists each juror's view regarding liability and damages. After the verdict or special report has been returned, counsel meets with the adjudicating official to discuss the verdict and establish a timetable for settlement negotiations.

Early neutral evaluation

Early neutral evaluation is an informal process by which a neutral intermediary is appointed to hear facts and arguments by the parties. In some jurisdictions, early neutral evaluation is a court-ordered alternative dispute resolution technique, the option of hiring a neutral intermediary or having the court appoint one.

After the hearing, the intermediary evaluates the parties' strengths and weaknesses and potential exposure to liability for money damages. The parties, counsel, and intermediary then engage in discussions designed to assist the parties in identifying the agreed-upon facts, isolating the issues in dispute, locating areas in which further investigation would be helpful, and devising a plan streamlining the investigative process. Settlement negotiations and mediation may follow, but only if the parties desire.

The objective of an early neutral evaluation is to obtain an initial assessment of the dispute by an objective intermediary with sufficient knowledge and experience to sift through the facts and issues and find the ground shared by the parties and the ground separating them. Much like in the other forms of alternative dispute resolution, the success of early neutral evaluation depends mainly on the party's credence in the process. It also depends in large part on the disputants' willingness to compromise and settle the dispute. Nevertheless, successful early neutral evaluations can lead directly to meaningful negotiations.

Alternative dispute resolution and civil litigation

The procedures and techniques discussed are the most common methods of ADR. However, despite its success over the past three decades, ADR is not the appropriate choice for all legal disputes. Many individuals and entities still resist ADR because it lacks the substantive, procedural, and evidentiary protections of formal civil litigation.

For example, parties to ADR typically waive their rights to object to evidence that might be deemed inadmissible under the court's rules. Hearsay evidence is a typical example of evidence that the parties and intermediaries consider in ADR forums but is generally excluded from civil trials. For example, suppose a disputant believes that they would be sacrificing too many rights and protections by waiving civil litigation formalities. In that case, ADR will not be the appropriate method of dispute resolution.

Exhibit 1: Complaint

UNITED STATES DISTRICT COURT FOR THE
EASTERN DISTRICT OF VIRGINIA

Civil Action No. 20-CV-1234

John Able,	)	
Plaintiff	)	COMPLAINT
v.	)	
Joseph Baker,	)	
Defendant	)	

1. Jurisdiction is founded on 28 U.S.C. § 1332. Plaintiff is a citizen of the state of Virginia. Defendant is a citizen of the state of Maryland. The amount in controversy exceeds $75,000, exclusive of interest and costs.

2. On January 12, 1999, the plaintiff was driving east on Virginia Beach Boulevard in Virginia Beach, Virginia. Plaintiff entered the intersection of Virginia Beach Boulevard and Witchduck Road when the traffic light directing eastbound Virginia Beach Boulevard traffic through the intersection was green.

3. While the plaintiff's car was in the intersection, the defendant, driving north on Witchduck Road, negligently drove his car into the intersection and the plaintiff's automobile.

4. As a result of the defendant's negligence, the plaintiff suffered physical injuries, including broken bones, muscle, ligament, tendon damage, bruises, and cuts. Plaintiff also suffered pain and emotional distress. Plaintiff required treatment at a hospital and was forced to be absent for two weeks from his job. Plaintiff also incurred expenses for physical therapy and continuing medical treatment.

Wherefore, the plaintiff demands judgment against the defendant for $650,000 plus costs and any other relief the court deems just in the circumstances.

Dated: July 25, 2020

Gordon Smith
Jones, Smith & Black
123 Granby Street
Norfolk, VA
(100) 100-1111
Attorneys for Plaintiff

Exhibit 2: Summons

UNITED STATES DISTRICT COURT FOR THE

EASTERN DISTRICT OF VIRGINIA

Civil Action No. 20-CV-1234

John Able,	)	
Plaintiff	)	SUMMONS
v.	)	
Joseph Baker,	)	
Defendant	)	

To the above named Defendant:

You are hereby summoned and required to serve upon Gordon Howe, 123 Granby Street, Norfolk, Virginia, plaintiff's attorney, an answer to the complaint served upon you with this summons, within 20 days after service of this summons upon you, exclusive of the day of service. If you fail to answer by that time, judgment by default will be taken against you for the relief demanded in the complaint.

[s]___________________________

Clerk of Court

[Seal of the U.S. District Court for the

Eastern District of Virginia]

Dated: July 25, 2020

Exhibit 3: Answer

UNITED STATES DISTRICT COURT FOR THE

EASTERN DISTRICT OF VIRGINIA

Civil Action No. 20-CV-1234

John Able,	)	
Plaintiff	)	ANSWER
v.	)	
Joseph Baker,	)	
Defendant	)	

1. Defendant admits the allegations in paragraph 1 of the plaintiff's complaint.

2. Defendant admits that plaintiff was driving east on Virginia Beach Boulevard. Defendant has insufficient information to admit or deny the other allegations in paragraph 2.

3. Defendant denies the allegations in paragraph 3.

4. Defendant denies that plaintiff suffered injury as a result of any negligence by the defendant. Defendant has insufficient information to admit or deny the remaining allegations in paragraph 4.

Wherefore, defendant asks that plaintiff take nothing by this action, plus any other relief the court deems.

Dated: September 3, 2020

                                          Austin Powers

                                          Powers & Evil

                                          321 Granby Street

                                          Norfolk, VA

                                          (100) 000-0000

                                          Attorneys for Defendant

Exhibit 4: Judgment in a civil case

UNITED STATES DISTRICT COURT FOR THE

EASTERN DISTRICT OF VIRGINIA

Civil Action No. 20-CV-1234

John Able,	)	
Plaintiff	)	JUDGMENT IN A CIVIL CASE
v.	)	
Joseph Baker,	)	
Defendant	)	

Judgment is to be entered as follows:

Upon the jury's verdict, plaintiff John Able is awarded $200,000 damages from defendant, Joseph Baker, plus costs.

Dated: February 8, 2021

[s] ___________________________

Clerk of Court

Exhibit 5: Notice of appeal

UNITED STATES DISTRICT COURT FOR THE

EASTERN DISTRICT OF VIRGINIA

Civil Action No. 20-CV-1234

John Able,	)	
Plaintiff	)	NOTICE OF APPEAL
v.	)	
Joseph Baker,	)	
Defendant	)	

Defendant gives notice that he is appealing the court's judgment entered February 8, 2000.

Dated: February 28, 2021

____

Austin Powers

Powers & Evil

321 Granby Street

Norfolk, VA

(100) 000-0000

Attorneys for Defendant

Exhibit 6: Docket

UNITED STATES DISTRICT COURT FOR THE
EASTERN DISTRICT OF VIRGINIA

Civil Action No. 20-CV-1234

John Able, 　　　Plaintiff 　　　v. Joseph Baker, 　　　Defendant	)))))

DOCKET

7/25/20 – Plaintiff files Complaint; Summons issues.

8/23/20 – Return of Summons, Defendant served summons and complaint.

9/3/20 – Defendant files Answer.

　　　[Omissions up to judgment]

2/8/21 – Enter Judgment: Upon the jury's verdict, plaintiff John Able is awarded $300,000 damages from defendant, Joseph Baker, plus costs.

2/28/21 – Defendant files Notice of appeal.

Appendix

History of American law

As the American colonies were settled, they relied on the English legal system, known as *common law*.

Principles announced in case decisions are precedent (i.e., guidance) for judges deciding similar disputes.

Three separate courts were established to resolve disputes:

1) Law courts

   Before 1066, the local lord was in charge of the locality and resolved disputes as he saw fit.

   After the Norman Conquest (1066), these localized courts were replaced with a uniform law system.

   Followers of William the Conqueror were appointed to administer justice uniformly in courts of law.

   The focus was on procedure rather than the merits of the case.

   Damages were in the form of monetary relief or compensation.

2) Chancery (equity) courts

   Addressed situations where the result in the law court was unfair or could not be corrected by monetary awards (e.g., injunction).

   Equity courts focus on the merits of the case rather than strict adherence to procedure.

   Remedies are shaped to fit each dispute.

3) Merchant courts for trade disputes

   Rules were developed by the merchants who traveled throughout Europe to resolve disputes that uniformly arose from trade.

   Rules evolved to the law of merchants based upon common trade practice and usage.

   Eventually, separate merchant courts adjudicated trade disputes.

Adoption of English common law in America

Except for Louisiana, states base their legal systems primarily on English common law.

The law, equity, and merchant courts have been merged.

Most U.S. courts permit the aggrieved party to seek both law (i.e., money damages) and equitable remedies (i.e., injunctions, declaratory judgments).

Civil codes and statutory laws

The civil law system models the Romano-Germanic codified legal system.

Civil code and parliamentary statutes proclaim and interpret the law as the sole sources of the law.

The adjudication of a case is applying the code or statutes to a specific set of facts.

In some civil law countries, court decisions do not have the force of law unless codified into law.

Functions of the law

Although a precise definition of law is complex, it is generally agreed that law must be obeyed and followed, and disobedience is subject to penalty.

The law is often described by the function it serves within a society. The primary functions served by the law in this country are to:

1) keep the peace, which includes making certain activities crimes;

2) shape moral standards, which includes prohibiting certain activities that

   society considers inappropriate or wrong;

3) promote social justice, such as enacting laws that prohibit wrongful

   discrimination;

4) maintain the status quo, which includes passing laws preventing the forceful

   overthrow of the government;

5) facilitate orderly change, such as passing statutes after public debate and input;

6) facilitate planning, commercial laws allowing businesses to plan and

   allocate resources;

7) provide a basis for compromise since 90 percent of lawsuits are settled
   prior to trial; and

8) maximize individual freedom, evidenced by the Bill of Rights.

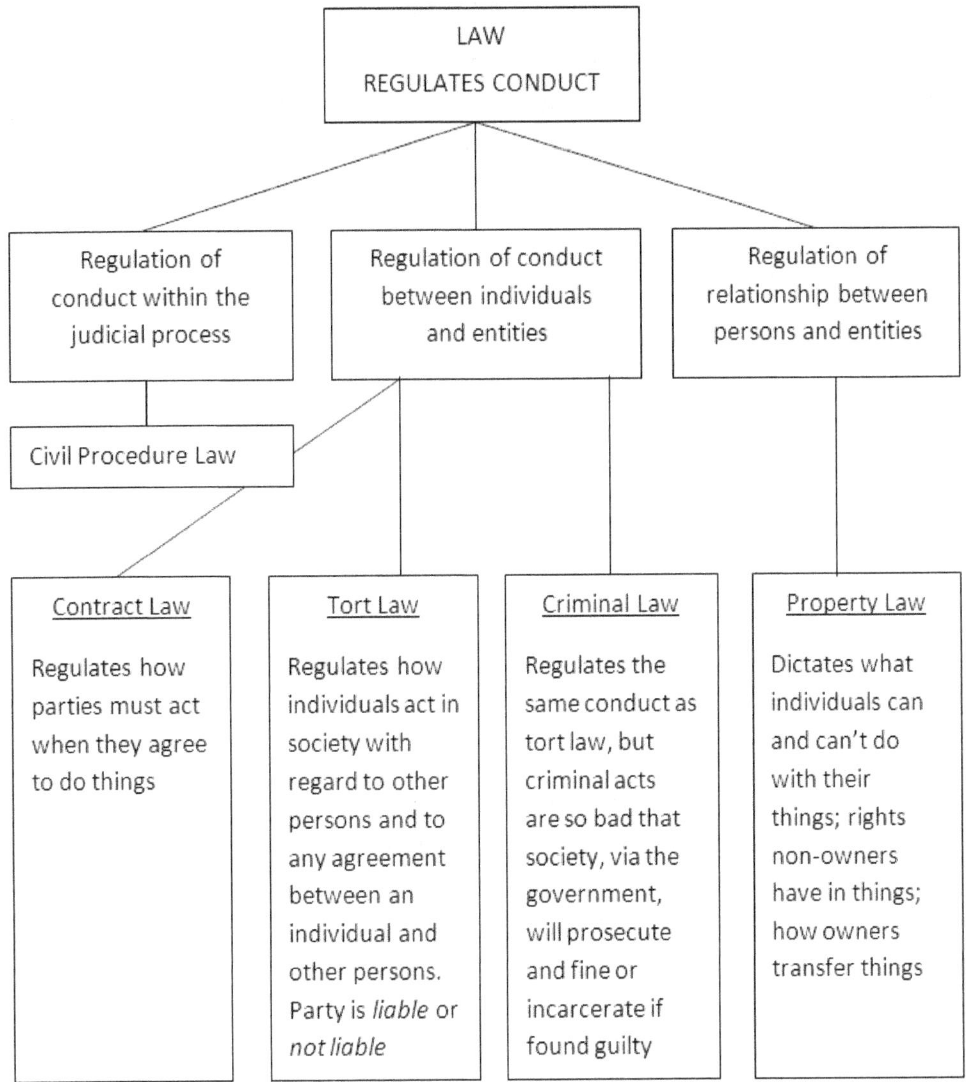

LAW
REGULATES CONDUCT

Regulation of conduct within the judicial process

Regulation of conduct between individuals and entities

Regulation of relationship between persons and entities

Civil Procedure Law

Contract Law

Regulates how parties must act when they agree to do things

Tort Law

Regulates how individuals act in society with regard to other persons and to any agreement between an individual and other persons. Party is liable or not liable

Criminal Law

Regulates the same conduct as tort law, but criminal acts are so bad that society, via the government, will prosecute and fine or incarcerate if found guilty

Property Law

Dictates what individuals can and can't do with their things; rights non-owners have in things; how owners transfer things

Sources of United States law

The foundational source of law in the United States is the U.S. Constitution, which establishes the federal government and enumerates its powers. The U.S. Constitution is *the supreme law of the land*. Therefore, any local, state, or federal law conflicting with the Constitution is void and unenforceable.

Powers not given to the federal government are reserved to the states. State constitutions establish state governments and enumerate their powers.

Treaties are international agreements entered into with other countries, executed by the President with *advice and consent* from the Senate.

Statutes and *ordinances* are codified laws and are created by legislative bodies. Statutes are interpreted and enforced by two types of agency action.

> *Rulemaking* – the adoption of rules and regulations by the agency defining the requirements of a statute. For example, the definition of gross income under the statute is less than one page, but the IRS regulations for this term are dozens of pages.

> *Decisionmaking* – agencies resolve disputes arising under the rules, regulations, and authorizing statute.

Codified laws establish courses of conduct that covered parties must follow. They are written laws (i.e., statutes) enacted by the legislative branch to define acceptable conduct by its citizens. For example, U.S. Congress empowered the commerce clause to regulate commerce between the states and with the Indian nations (e.g., antitrust, bankruptcy). The state legislature has similar power to regulate activity within its borders (e.g., workers compensation, uniform commercial, licenses). State legislatures delegate some power to municipalities, school districts, and others. (e.g., ordinances for building codes, zoning, traffic).

Administrative rules and regulations come from bureaucracies created by the legislative and executive branches of government. Agencies interpret and enforce statutes enacted by legislation (e.g., Congress enacted a statute authorizing the collection of income taxes). For example, the IRS is the administrative agency charged with interpreting and enforcing the income tax statute.

Executive orders are issued by the President and state governors and regulate the conduct of those on whom the executive orders are focused.

Judicial decisions are written opinions of a judge or justice deciding the dispute before setting forth the reasons for the decision. These decisions resolve the dispute and serve as a precedent for the resolution of a future similar dispute. Judicial decisions are often created by appellate courts that resolve legal controversies. An appellate court issues decisions that state the holding of the case and the rationale used by the court in reaching that decision.

Priority of law in the United States

1) U.S. Constitution takes precedence over all other laws (i.e., *the supreme law of the land*).

2) Federal statutes take precedence over federal regulations.

3) Federal law takes precedence over state law, where the state law conflicts.

4) State constitution represents the highest authority in the state, state statutes, then state regulations.

Values-based law

Moral values address fundamental questions of right and wrong. For example, laws against murder protect life. However, not every immoral act breaks the law (e.g., lying to a friend).

Economic values address the accumulation, preservation, use, and distribution of wealth. For example, laws against shoplifting protect property. In addition, the law encourages homeownership by giving tax benefits to incentivize people to borrow and buy a home.

Political values address the relationship between government and individuals (e.g., voting, criminal law).

Social values address issues important to society (e.g., free public education).

Many laws combine values. For example, consider laws against theft. The laws address *moral* (e.g., stealing), *economic* (e.g., protection of property), *political* (punishment for violating criminal statutes), and *social issues* (e.g., respecting the property of others).

The doctrine of *stare decisis*

Court decisions become guidance or precedent for future cases. Lower courts must follow precedent set by higher courts.

The precedent of another jurisdiction does not bind courts in other jurisdictions.

Adherence to *stare decisis* promotes uniformity and predictability of the legal system.

Constitution of the United States of America

U.S. Constitution established a form of the federal government with three branches:

1) Legislative to enact laws – Congress consists of the House of Representatives and Senate.

2) Executive to enforce the laws – President, Vice President, and administrative agencies.

3) Judicial to interpret and determine the validity of laws – courts.

Powers given to the federal government are enumerated or designated powers set forth in the Constitution. All other powers not enumerated in the Constitution are reserved for the states. The emphasis is to protect the rights of individuals (i.e., civil liberties).

Federalism and delegated powers

Federalism – the power to govern is shared by one central or federal government and the 50 states

Delegated (or Enumerated) Powers – those powers set forth in the Constitution assigned to the federal government. Enumerated powers authorize the federal government to regulate specific national and international affairs.

Reserved Powers – those powers not delegated to the federal government are reserved for the states.

The doctrine of separation of powers

Article I establishes a bicameral legislature – establishes Congress.

1) House of Representatives, where each state has representation based on population.

2) Senate, where each state is represented equally with two Senators.

Article II establishes the offices of the President and Vice President and describes requirements and how elected.

Article III establishes a judiciary to hear and resolve legal disputes.

Checks and balances

Checks and balances are included in the federal government system so that no branch becomes too powerful.

1) Judiciary may examine the acts of the Congress and President to determine whether they comply with Constitution provisions.

2) President enters treaties with foreign nations with the advice and consent of the Senate.

Supremacy clause

The Constitution, treaties, federal laws, and regulations are the supreme law of the land.

To the extent state and local laws conflict with federal law, they are preempted.

Some areas of governance are exclusively the federal government's (e.g., postage, coining money, national defense).

Some areas of governance are concurrent where both the state and federal governments share powers (e.g., environmental protection).

Commerce clause

Congress granted the power to regulate trade with foreign governments, between states, and with the Indian nations.

Native Americans

1) At the time of its founding, the colonies (states), in the U.S. Constitution, delegated to the federal government the authority to regulate commerce with the Indian tribes.

2) Applicable to the original thirteen states and the territory to become the United States of America.

Foreign Commerce

1) Federal government has the exclusive power to regulate commerce with foreign nations.

2) Typically through treaties negotiated and signed by the President with the consent of the Senate.

Interstate Commerce

1) Federal government the authority to regulate interstate commerce.

2) Originally interpreted, this clause means commerce that moved in interstate commerce.

3) Modern rule allows the federal government to regulate activities that affect interstate commerce.

4) This test subjects a substantial amount of business activity in the United States to federal regulation.

State Police Power

1) The retained powers of the states to govern within their borders are police power

2) The power to enact legislation for health, safety, welfare, morals, and aesthetics.

3) Includes those powers delegated to local municipalities (e.g., building regulations, zoning codes).

Dormant commerce clause

Prohibits state legislation that discriminates against interstate commerce.

Bill of Rights and other Amendments

The Bill of Rights is the first ten Amendments to the U.S. Constitution ratified in 1791 and guarantying fundamental rights reserved for the people.

Freedom of speech

The First Amendment *freedom of speech* protects the right of individuals to speak freely.

The first Amendment divides speech into three categories.

1) Fully protected speech is political speech (e.g., oral, written, symbolic) that the government may not prohibit or regulate (e.g., flag burning).

2) Limited protected speech: may not be prohibited but may be regulated for time, place, and manner.

    a. Offensive speech may be regulated (i.e., FCC regulation of radio and television programs).

    b. Commercial speech such as advertising cannot be prohibited but may be restricted to placement for safety or aesthetic reasons.

3) Unprotected speech: may be prohibited or banned by the government.

    a. Common examples include yelling "fire!" in a crowded place, fighting words, and defamation.

    b. One complicated issue to define is obscenity; what may be obscene may be acceptable to another.

    c. Obscene speech is a category of speech unprotected by the First Amendment.

    d. Obscenity laws prohibit lewd, filthy, or disgusting words or pictures.

Free speech in cyberspace

The Supreme Court held that the Internet be given the highest level of First Amendment free-speech protections.

As a participatory form of mass speech, the Internet deserves the highest protection from government intrusion.

Because the Internet is a global medium, there is no way to prevent indecent material from abroad.

Freedom of religion

The Establishment clause prohibits the federal government from establishing a state religion and has been interpreted to prohibit promoting one religion over another.

The Free Exercise clause prohibits the federal government from interfering with the rights of the individual to worship as desired unless it involves human or animal sacrifice.

Due process clause

No person shall be deprived of life, liberty, or property without due process of law.

Due process applies to the federal government (via the 5th Amendment) and the state and local governments (via the 14th Amendment).

Substantive due process:

1) Requires that laws enacted by the government be clear on their face and not overly broad.

2) Test whether a "reasonable person" could understand the law to comply with it.

Procedural due process:

> The government must give notice and a hearing (i.e., opportunity to be heard) to the individual of legal action taken against them.

Equal protection clause

Prohibits state, local and federal governments from denying persons equal protection of the law.

Laws that classify and treat similarly situated persons differently violate the equal protection clause.

Three levels of tests developed by the Supreme Court to address equal protection and what has come to be known as the anti-discrimination provision of the Constitution

Strict scrutiny – a regulation that classifies individuals based upon a suspect class (race) generally will not be found constitutional (e.g., granting federal benefit to one race violates Equal Protection).

Intermediate scrutiny – regulation related to protected classes (age or sex) will be permissible so long as reasonably related to a legitimate government purpose (e.g., requiring government engineers to be men violates Equal Protection).

Rational basis – regulations of classes other than suspect and protected will be permissible where the is a justifiable reason for the law (e.g., subsidies to a farmer).

Notes for active learning

U.S. Court Systems – Federal and State Courts

There are two kinds of courts in the USA – federal courts and state courts.

Federal courts are established under the U.S. Constitution by Congress to decide disputes involving the Constitution and laws passed by Congress. A state establishes state and local courts (within states, local courts are established by cities, counties, and other municipalities).

Jurisdiction of federal and state courts

The differences between federal courts and state courts are defined by jurisdiction.[1] Jurisdiction refers to the kinds of cases that a particular court is authorized to hear and adjudicate (i.e., the pronouncement of a legally binding judgment upon the parties to the dispute).

Federal court jurisdiction is limited to the types of cases listed in the Constitution and specifically provided by Congress. For the most part, federal courts only hear:

- cases in which the United States is a party[2];

- cases involving violations of the U.S. Constitution or federal laws (under federal-question jurisdiction[3]);

- cases between citizens of different states if the amount in controversy *exceeds* $75,000 (under diversity jurisdiction[4]); and

- bankruptcy, copyright, patent, and maritime law cases.

State courts, in contrast, have broad jurisdiction, so the cases individual citizens are likely to be involved in (e.g., robberies, traffic violations, contracts, and family disputes) are usually heard and decided in state courts. The only cases state courts are not allowed to hear are lawsuits against the United States and those involving certain specific federal laws: criminal, antitrust, bankruptcy, patent, copyright, and some maritime law cases.

In many cases, both federal and state courts have jurisdiction whereby the plaintiff (i.e., the party initiating the suit) can choose whether to file their claim in state or federal court.

Criminal cases involving federal laws can be tried only in federal court, but most criminal cases involve violations of state law and are tried in state court. Robbery is a crime, but what law makes it is a crime? Except for certain exceptions, state laws, not federal laws, make robbery a crime. There are only a few federal laws about robbery, such as the law that makes it a federal crime to rob a bank whose deposits are insured by a federal agency. Examples of other federal crimes are the transport of illegal drugs into the country or across state lines and using the U.S. mail system to defraud consumers.

Crimes committed on federal property (e.g., national parks or military reservations) are prosecuted in federal court.

Federal courts may hear cases concerning state laws if the issue is whether the state law violates the federal Constitution. Suppose a state law forbids slaughtering animals outside of certain limited areas. A neighborhood association brings a case in state court against a defendant who sacrifices chickens in their backyard. When the court issues an order (i.e., an injunction[5]) forbidding the defendant from further sacrifices, the defendant challenges the state law in federal court as an unconstitutional infringement of religious freedom.

Some conduct is illegal under both federal and state laws. For example, federal laws prohibit employment discrimination, and the states have added additional legal restrictions. A person can file their claim in either federal or state court under federal law or federal and state laws. A case that only involves a state law can be brought only in state court.

Appeals for review of actions by federal administrative agencies are federal civil cases.

For example, if the Environmental Protection Agency, over the objection of area residents, issued a permit to a paper mill to discharge water used in its milling process into the Scenic River, the residents may appeal and have the federal court of appeals review the agency's decision.

[1] *jurisdiction* – 1) the legal authority of a court to hear and decide specific types of case; 2) the geographic area over which the court has the authority to decide cases.

[2] *parties* – the plaintiff and the defendant in a lawsuit.

[3] *federal-question jurisdiction* – the federal district courts' authorization to hear and decide cases arising under the Constitution, laws, or treaties of the United States.

[4] *diversity jurisdiction* – the federal district courts' authority to hear and decide civil cases involving plaintiffs and defendants who are citizens of different states (or U.S. citizens and foreign nationals) and meet specific statutory requirements.

[5] *injunction* – a judge's order that a party takes or refrain from taking a particular action. An injunction may be preliminary until the outcome of a case is determined or permanent.

Organization of the federal courts

Congress has divided the country into 94 federal judicial districts, with each having a U.S. district court. The U.S. district courts are the federal trial courts -- where federal cases are tried, witnesses testify, and juries serve.

Each district has a U.S. bankruptcy court, which is part of the district court that administers the U.S. bankruptcy laws.

Congress uses state boundaries to help define the districts. Some districts cover an entire state, like Idaho. Other districts cover just part of a state, like the Northern District of California. Congress placed each of the ninety-four districts in one of twelve regional circuits whereby each circuit has a court of appeals. The losing party can petition the court of appeals to review the case to determine if the district judge applied the law correctly.

There is a U.S. Court of Appeals for the Federal Circuit, whose jurisdiction is defined by subject matter rather than geography. It hears appeals from certain courts and agencies, such as the U.S. Court of International Trade, the U.S. Court of Federal Claims, and the U.S. Patent and Trademark Office, and certain types of cases from the district courts (mainly lawsuits claiming that patents have been infringed).

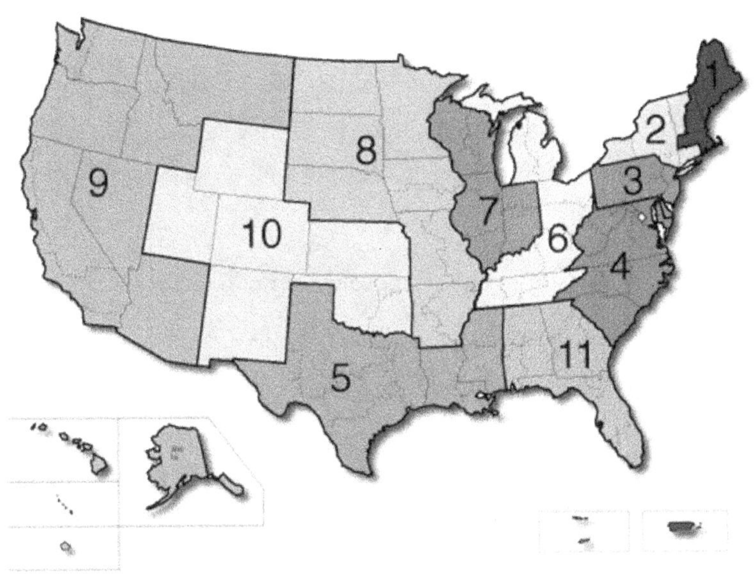

Twelve regional federal circuits

The Supreme Court in Washington, D.C., is the highest court in the nation. The losing party can petition in a case in the court of appeals (or, sometimes, in a state supreme court), can petition the Supreme Court to hear an appeal.

Unlike a court of appeals, the Supreme Court does not have to hear the case. The Supreme Court hears only a small percentage of the cases it is asked to review.

The importance of judicial independence

The founders of the United States recognized that the judicial branch must remain independent to fulfill its mission effectively and impartially. Article III of the Constitution protects certain types of judges by providing that they serve "during good behavior" and prohibits the reduction of their salary.

These constitutional protections allow judges to make unpopular decisions without fear of losing their jobs or having their pay cut.

For example, the Supreme Court's decision in *Brown v. Board of Education* in 1954 declared racial segregation in public schools to be unconstitutional. This decision was unpopular with large segments of society at that time. Some members of Congress even wanted to replace the judges who made the decision, but this Constitutional protection would not allow them to do so.

Article III judges

"Article III judge" denotes federal judges who under Article III of the Constitution are enabled to exercise "the judicial power of the United States" without fear of losing their jobs. They serve for "good Behaviour," which means they can be removed from office only by the rare impeachment and conviction process.

Article III further provides that their compensation cannot be reduced. From a practical standpoint, almost all of these judges hold office for as long as they wish. "Article III judges" are those on the U.S. Supreme Court, the federal courts of appeals and district courts, and the U.S. Court of International Trade.

Constitutional protections for the judiciary

Federal judges appointed under Article III of the Constitution are guaranteed what amounts to life tenure and a fixed salary, not to be afraid to make an unpopular decision.

For example, in *Gregg v. Georgia*, the Supreme Court said it is constitutional for the federal and state governments to impose the death penalty if the statute is carefully drafted to provide adequate safeguards. Even though some people are opposed to the death penalty, Article III protections allowed the Judge to decide without fear of reciprocity.

The constitutional protection that gives federal judges the freedom and independence to make decisions politically and socially unpopular is a fundamental element of our democracy.

According to the Declaration of Independence, one reason the American colonies wanted to separate from England was that King George III "made judges dependent on his/her will alone, for the tenure of their offices, and the amount and payment of their salaries."

Federal judges other than enumerated in Article III

Bankruptcy judges and magistrate judges conduct some of the proceedings held in federal courts. Bankruptcy judges handle almost all bankruptcy matters in bankruptcy courts technically included in the district courts but function as separate entities.

Magistrate judges carry out various responsibilities in the district courts and often help prepare the district judges' cases for trial. They also may preside over criminal misdemeanor trials and may preside over civil trials when both parties agree to have the case heard by a magistrate judge instead of a district judge.

Unlike district judges, bankruptcy and magistrate judges do not exercise "the judicial power of the United States" but perform duties delegated to them by district judges. Bankruptcy and magistrate judges serve for fourteen and eight-year terms, respectively, rather than "during good Behaviour."

Bankruptcy judges and magistrate judges don't have the same protections as judges appointed under Article III of the Constitution. Bankruptcy judges, in contrast, may be removed from office by circuit judicial councils, and magistrate judges may be removed by the district judges of the magistrate judge's district.

Courts and judges

Congress authorizes a set number of judge positions, or judgeships, for each court level. Since the 1869 "Circuit Judges Act," Congress mandated that the Supreme Court would consist of 9 justices. As of 2021, it had mandated 179 court of appeals judgeships and 678 district court judgeships. (In 1950, there were 65 courts of appeals and 212 district judgeships).

As of 2018, Congress mandated 350 bankruptcy judgeships and about 551 full-time and part-time magistrate judgeships. All judgeships are rarely filled at any one time as judges die or retire, causing vacancies until judges are appointed to replace them. In addition to judges in these positions, retired judges continue to perform some judicial work.

Federal judges and judgeships

Supreme Court justices and the court of appeals and district judges are appointed to office by the President, with the approval of the U.S. Senate. Presidents most often appoint judges who are members, or at least supportive, of their political party, but that does not mean that judges are given appointments solely for partisan reasons.

The professional qualifications of prospective federal judges are rigorously evaluated by the Department of Justice (DOJ), which consults with others, such as lawyers who can evaluate the prospect's abilities. The Senate Judiciary Committee undertakes a separate examination of the nominees.

Magistrate judges and bankruptcy judges are not appointed by the President or subject to Congress's approval. The court of appeals in each circuit appoints bankruptcy judges for fourteen-year terms. District courts appoint magistrate judges for eight-year terms.

Qualifications for becoming a federal judge

Although there are almost no formal qualifications for federal judges, there are some informal ones. For example, while magistrate judges and bankruptcy judges are required by statute to be lawyers, there is no requirement that district judges, circuit judges, or Supreme Court justices be lawyers.

However, there is no legal precedent for a president to nominate someone who is not a lawyer. Before their appointment, most judges were private attorneys, but many were judges in state courts or other federal courts. Some were government attorneys, and a few were law professors.

Ethical standards for judges

Judges follow the ethical standards set out in the *Code of Conduct for United States Judges*, which contains guidelines to help them avoid situations that might limit their ability to be fair--or that might make it appear to others that their fairness is in question. It tells them, for example, to be careful not to do anything that might cause people to think they would favor one side in a case over another, such as giving speeches that urge voters to pick one candidate over another for public office or asking people to contribute money to civic organizations.

Additionally, Congress has enacted laws telling judges to withdraw or recuse themselves from any case in which a close relative is a party or in which they have any financial interest, even one share of stock.

Congress requires judges to file an annual financial disclosure form, so that their stock holdings, board memberships, and other financial interests are a matter of public record.

Congress has also enacted a law that allows anyone to file a complaint alleging that a judge (other than a Supreme Court justice) has engaged in conduct "prejudicial to the effective and expeditious administration of the business of the courts" or that a judge has a mental or physical disability that makes him/her unable to discharge the duties of the office adequately.

A complaint is filed with the clerk of the court of appeals of the judge's circuit and considered by the chief judge of the court of appeals. If the chief judge believes the complaint deserves attention, the chief judge appoints a special committee of the circuit judicial council to investigate.

If the committee concludes that the complaint is valid, it may recommend various actions, such as temporarily removing the judge from hearing cases, but it may not recommend that an Article III judge be removed from office. Only Congress may do that, through the impeachment process.

Chief Judges dismiss the great majority of complaints filed under this law because the complaints involve judges' decisions in particular cases. This law may not be used to complain about decisions, even what may appear to be a very wrong decision or very unfair treatment of a party in a case.

Parties in a lawsuit who believe the judge issued an incorrect ruling may appeal the case to a higher court, under the rules of procedure.

Senior judge status

Most federal judges retire from full-time service at around sixty-five or seventy years of age and become senior judges. Senior judges are still federal judges, eligible to earn their full salary and to continue hearing cases if they and their colleagues want them to do so, but they usually maintain a reduced caseload.

Full-time judges are known as active judges.

Docket assignments

Each court, with more than one judge, must determine a procedure for assigning cases to judges.

Most district and bankruptcy courts use random assignment, which helps to ensure a fair distribution of cases and prevents "judge shopping," which refers to parties' attempts to have their cases heard by the judge whom they believe will act most favorably.

Other courts assign cases by rotation, subject matter, or geographic division of the court.

In courts of appeals, cases are usually assigned by random means to temporary three-judge panels.

Notes for active learning

How Civil Cases Move Through the Federal Courts

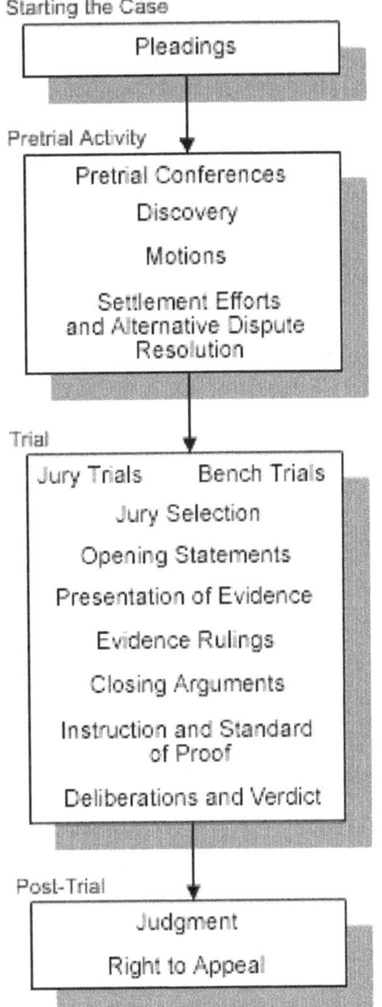

A federal civil case begins when a person, or their legal representative, files a paper with the clerk of the court that asserts another person's wrongful act injured the person. In legal terminology, the plaintiff files a *complaint* against the defendant.

The defendant files an *answer* to the complaint. These written statements of the party's positions are called pleadings. In some circumstances, the defendant may file a *motion* instead of an answer; the motion asks the court to take some action, such as dismiss the case or require the plaintiff to explain more clearly what the lawsuit is about.

Jury trials

In a jury trial, the jury decides what happened, and to apply the legal standards, the judge tells them to apply to reach a verdict. The plaintiff presents evidence supporting its view of the case, and the defendant presents evidence rebutting the plaintiff's evidence or supporting its view of the case. From these presentations, the jury must decide what happened and applied the law to those facts.

The jury never decides what law applies to the case; that is the role of the judge. For example, in a discrimination case where the plaintiff alleged that their workplace was hostile, the judge tells the jury the legal standard for a hostile environment.

The jury would have to decide whether the plaintiff's description of events was true and whether those events met the legal standard. A trial jury, or petit jury, may consist of six to twelve jurors in a civil case.

Bench trials

If the parties agree not to have a *jury trial* and leave the fact-finding to the judge, the trial is a *bench trial*. In bench and jury trials, the judge ensures the correct legal standards are followed.

In contrast to a jury trial, the judge decides the facts and renders the verdict in a *bench trial*.

For example, in a discrimination case in which the plaintiff alleged a hostile environment, the judge would determine the legal standard for a hostile environment and decide whether the plaintiff's description of events was true and whether those events met the legal standard.

Some kinds of cases always have bench trials. For example, there is never a jury trial if the plaintiff is seeking an injunction, an order from the judge that the defendant does, or stop doing something, as opposed to monetary damages.

Some statutes provide that a judge must decide the facts in certain types of cases.

Jury selection

A jury trial begins with the selection of jurors. Citizens are selected for jury service through a process set out in laws passed by Congress and in the federal rules of procedure.

First, citizens are called to court to be available to serve on juries. These citizens are selected at random from sources, in most districts, lists of registered voters, which may be augmented by other sources, such as lists of licensed drivers in the judicial district.

The judge and the lawyers choose who will serve on the jury.

To choose the jurors, the judge and sometimes the lawyers ask prospective jurors questions to determine if they will decide the case fairly, a process known as *voir dire*.

The lawyers may request that the judge excuse jurors they think may not be impartial, such as those who know a party in the case or who have had an experience that might make them favor one side over the other. These requests for rejecting jurors are *challenges for cause*.

The lawyers may request that the judge excuse a certain number of jurors without reason; these requests are *peremptory challenges*.

Instructions and standard of proof

Following the closing arguments, the judge gives instructions to the jury, explaining the relevant law, how the law applies to the case, and what questions the jury must decide.

How sure do jurors have to be before they reach a verdict? One important instruction the judge gives the jury is the standard of proof they must follow in deciding the case.

The courts, through their decisions, and Congress, through statutes, have established standards by which facts must be proven in criminal and civil cases.

In civil cases, to decide for the plaintiff, the jury must determine by a *preponderance of the evidence* that the defendant failed to perform a legal duty and violated the plaintiff's rights. A preponderance of the evidence means that, based on the evidence, the evidence favors the plaintiff more (even if only slightly) than it favors the defendant.

If the evidence in favor of the plaintiff could be placed on one side of a scale and that in favor of the defendant on the other, the plaintiff would win if the evidence in favor of the plaintiff was heavy enough to tip the scale. If the two sides were even, or if the scale tipped for the defendant, the defendant would win.

Judgment

In civil cases, if the jury (or judge) decides in favor of the plaintiff, the result usually is that the defendant must pay the plaintiff money or damages. The judge orders the defendant to pay the decided amount. Sometimes the defendant is ordered to take some specific action that will restore the plaintiff's rights. If the defendant wins the case, there is nothing more the trial court needs to do as the case is disposed of and the defendant is held not liable.

Right to appeal

The losing party in a federal civil case has a right to appeal the verdict to the U.S. court of appeals (i.e., Federal Circuit Courts) and ask the court to review the case to determine whether the trial was conducted properly. The losing party in the state trial court has a right to appeal the verdict to the state court of appeal.

The grounds for appeal usually are that the federal district (or state) judge made an error, either in the procedure (e.g., admitting improper evidence) or interpreting the law. The government may appeal in civil cases, as any other party may. Neither party may appeal if there was no trial -- parties settled their civil case out of court.

Notes for active learning

How Criminal Cases Move Through the Federal Courts

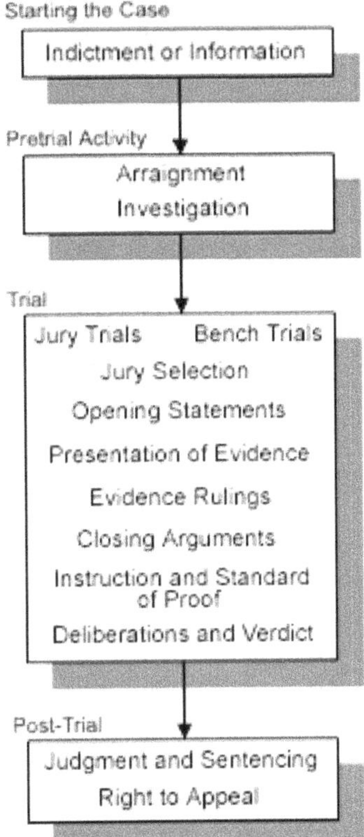

Indictment or information

A criminal case formally begins with an indictment or information, which is a formal accusation that a person committed a crime.

An indictment may be obtained when a lawyer (i.e., prosecutor) for the executive branch of the U.S. government (i.e., U.S. attorney or assistant U.S. attorney) present evidence to a federal grand jury that, according to the government, indicates a person committed a crime.

The U.S. attorney tries to convince the grand jury that there is enough evidence to show that the person probably committed the crime and should be formally accused. If the grand jury agrees, it issues an indictment.

A grand jury is different from a trial jury or petit jury.

A grand jury determines whether the person may be tried for a crime; a petit jury listens to the evidence presented at the trial and determines whether the defendant is guilty.

Petit is French for "small"; petit juries usually consist of twelve jurors in criminal cases.

Grand is French for "large"; grand juries have from sixteen to twenty-three jurors.

Grand jury indictments are most often used for *felonies* (i.e., punishable by imprisonment of more than a year or by death) such as bank robberies or sales of illegal drugs.

Grand jury indictments are not necessary to prosecute *misdemeanors* (i.e., less serious than a felony but more serious than an infraction) and are necessary for felonies.

For lesser crimes, the U.S. attorney issues an *information* that substitutes for an indictment. For example, speeding on a highway in a national park is a misdemeanor.

An information is used when a defendant waives an indictment by a grand jury.

Arraignment

After the grand jury issues the indictment, the accused (i.e., defendant) is summoned to court or arrested (if not already in custody). The next step is an arraignment, a proceeding in which the defendant is brought before a judge, told of the charges they are accused of, and asked to plead guilty or not guilty. If the defendant's plea is guilty, a time is set for the defendant to return to court to be sentenced.

If the defendant pleads "not guilty," the time is set for the trial.

A defendant may enter a plea bargain with the prosecution--usually by agreeing to plead guilty to some but not all charges or lesser charges. The prosecution drops the remaining charges.

About nine out of ten defendants in criminal cases plead guilty.

Investigation

In a criminal case, a defense lawyer conducts a thorough investigation before trial, interviewing witnesses, visiting the crime scene, and examining physical evidence. An important part of this investigation is determining whether the evidence the government plans to use to prove its case was obtained legally.

The Fourth Amendment to the Constitution forbids unreasonable searches and seizures. To enforce this protection, the Supreme Court has decided that illegally seized evidence cannot be used at trial for most purposes.

For example, if the police seize evidence from a defendant's home without a search warrant, the lawyer for the defendant can ask the court to exclude the evidence from use at trial. The court holds a hearing to determine whether the search was unreasonable.

If the court rules that key evidence was seized illegally and cannot be used, the government often drops the charges against the defendant.

If the government has a strong case and the court ruled that the evidence was obtained legally, the defendant may decide to plead guilty rather than go to trial, where a conviction is likely.

Deliberations and verdict

After receiving its instructions from the judge, the jury retires to the jury room to discuss the evidence and reach a verdict (a decision on the factual issues). A criminal jury verdict must be unanimous; all jurors must agree that the defendant is guilty or not guilty.

If the jurors cannot agree, the judge declares a mistrial, and the prosecutor must decide whether to ask the court to dismiss the case or have it presented to another jury.

Judgment and sentencing

In federal criminal cases, if the jury (or judge, if there is no jury) decides that the defendant is guilty, the judge sets a date for a sentencing hearing. In federal criminal cases, the jury does not decide whether the defendant will go to prison or for how long; the judge does.

In federal death penalty cases, the jury does decide whether the defendant will receive a death sentence. Sentencing statutes passed by Congress control the judge's sentencing decision. Additionally, judges use Sentencing Guidelines, issued by the U.S. Sentencing Commission, as a source of advice as to the proper sentence. The guidelines consider the nature of the offense and the offender's criminal history.

A presentence report, prepared by one of the court's probation officers, provides the judge with information about the offender and the offense, including the sentence recommended by the guidelines. After determining the sentence, the judge signs a judgment, including the plea, the verdict, and sentence.

Right to appeal

A defendant who is found guilty in a federal criminal trial has a right to appeal the decision to the U.S. court of appeals, that is, ask the court of appeals to review the case to determine whether the trial was conducted properly. The grounds for appeal are usually that the district judge is said to have made an error, either in a procedure (admitting improper evidence, for example) or interpreting the law.

A defendant who pled guilty may not appeal the conviction.

A defendant who pled guilty may have the right to appeal their sentence.

The government may not appeal if a defendant in a criminal case is found not guilty because the Double Jeopardy Clause of the Fifth Amendment to the Constitution provides that no person shall "be twice put in jeopardy of life or limb" for the same offense.

This reflects society's belief that, even if a subsequent trial might finally find a defendant guilty, it is not proper for the government to harass an acquitted defendant through repeated retrials.

However, the government may sometimes appeal a sentence.

Notes for active learning

How Civil and Criminal Appeals Move Through the Federal Courts

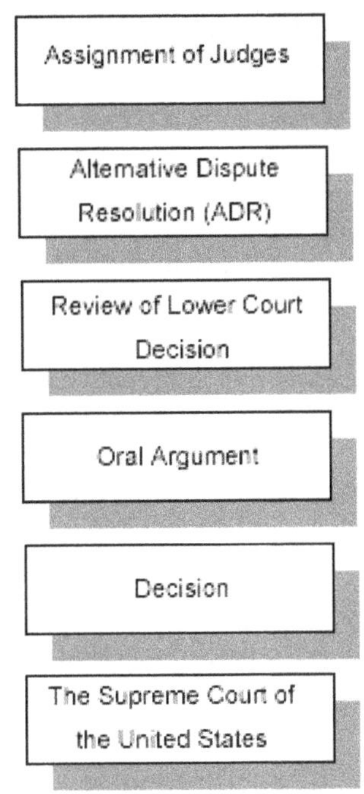

Assignment of judges

The courts of appeals usually assign cases to a panel of three judges. The panel decides the case for the entire court. Sometimes, when the parties request it or a question of unusual importance, the judges on the appeals court assemble *en banc* (a rare event).

Review of a lower court decision

In making its decision, the panel reviews key parts of the record. The record consists of the documents filed in the case at trial and the transcript of the trial proceedings. The panel learns about the lawyers' legal arguments from the lawyers' briefs.

Briefs are written documents that each side submits to explain its case and tell why the court should decide in its favor.

Oral argument

If the court permits oral argument, the lawyers for each side have a limited amount of time (typically between 15 to 30 minutes) to argue (i.e., advocate and explain) their case to the judges (or justices at the highest court in the jurisdiction) in a formal courtroom session. The judges (or justices for the highest court in the jurisdiction) frequently question the attorneys about the relevant law as it applies to the facts and issues in the case before them.

A court of appeals differs from the federal trial courts. There are no jurors, witnesses, or court reporters. The lawyers for each side, but not the parties, are usually present in the courtroom.

Decision

After the submission of briefs and oral arguments, the judges discuss the case privately, consider relevant *precedents* (court decisions from higher courts in prior cases with similar facts and legal issues), and reach a decision. Courts are required to follow precedents.

For example, a U.S. court of appeals must follow the U.S. Supreme Court's decisions; a district court must follow the decisions of the U.S. Supreme Court and the decisions of the court of appeals of its circuit.

Courts are influenced by decisions they are not required to follow, such as the decisions of other circuits. Courts follow precedent unless they set forth reasons for the diversion.

At least two of the three judges on the panel must agree on a decision. One judge who agrees with the decision is chosen to write an opinion, which announces and explains the decision.

If a judge on the panel disagrees with the majority's opinion, the judge may write a dissent, giving reasons for disagreeing.

Many appellate opinions are published in books of opinions, called reporters. The opinions are read carefully by other judges and lawyers looking for precedents to guide them in their cases.

The accumulated judicial opinions make up a body of law known as *case law*, which is usually an accurate predictor of how future cases will be decided.

For decisions that the judges believe are important to the parties and contribute little to the law, the appeals courts frequently use short, unsigned opinions that often are not published.

If the court of appeals decides that the trial judge incorrectly interpreted the law or followed incorrect procedures, it reverses the district court's decision.

For example, the court of appeals could hold that the district judge allowed the jury to base its decision on evidence that never should have been admitted, and thus the defendant cannot be guilty.

Most of the time, courts of appeals uphold, rather than the reverse, district court decisions.

Sometimes when a higher court reverses the decision of the district court, it sends the case back (i.e., *remand* the case) to the lower court for another trial.

For example, *Miranda v. Arizona* case (1966), the Supreme Court ruled 5-4 that Ernesto Miranda's confession could not be used as evidence because he had not been advised of his right to remain silent or of his right to have a lawyer present during questioning.

However, the government did have other evidence against him. The case was remanded for a new trial, in which the improperly obtained confession was not used as evidence, but the other evidence convicted Miranda.

The Supreme Court of the United States

The Supreme Court is the highest in the nation. It is a different kind of appeals court; its major function is not correcting errors made by trial judges but clarifying the law in cases of national importance or when lower courts disagree about interpreting the Constitution or federal laws.

The Supreme Court does not have to hear every case that it is asked to review. Each year, losing parties ask the Supreme Court to review about 8,000 cases.

Almost all cases come to the Court as a *petition for writ of certiorari*. The court selects only about 80 to 120 of the most significant cases to review with oral arguments.

Supreme Court decisions establish a precedent for interpreting the Constitution and federal laws; holdings that state and federal courts must follow.

The power of judicial review makes the Supreme Court's role in our government vital. Judicial review is the power of a court when deciding a case to declare that a law passed by a legislature or action by the executive branch is invalid because it is inconsistent with the Constitution.

Although district courts, courts of appeals, and state courts can exercise the power of judicial review, their decisions about federal law are always subject, on appeal, to review by the Supreme Court.

When the Supreme Court declares a law unconstitutional, its decision can only be overruled by a later decision of the Supreme Court or Amendment to the Constitution.

Seven of the twenty-seven Amendments to the Constitution have invalidated the decisions of the Supreme Court. However, most Supreme Court cases do not concern the constitutionality of laws, but the interpretation of laws passed by Congress.

Although Congress has steadily increased the number of district and appeals court judges over the years, the Supreme Court has remained the same size since 1869. It consists of a Chief Justice and eight associate justices.

Like the federal court of appeals and federal district judges, the Supreme Court justices are appointed by the President with the Senate's *advice and consent.*

Unlike the judges in the courts of appeals, Supreme Court justices never sit on panels. Absent recusal, nine justices hear cases, and a majority ruling decides cases.

The Supreme Court begins its annual session, or term, on the first Monday of October. The term lasts until the Court has announced its decisions in cases where it has heard an argument that term—usually late June or early July.

During the term, the Court, sitting for two weeks at a time, hears oral arguments on Monday through Wednesday and holds private conferences to discuss the cases, reach decisions, and begin preparing the written opinions that explain its decisions.

Most decisions and opinions are released in the late spring and early summer.

Notes for active learning

Standards of review for federal courts

Standard of review	*De novo*	Clearly erroneous	Abuse of discretion
Type of decision under review	Question of the law	Question of fact	Discretionary action
Lower-court decision maker	Trial judge	Trial judge	Trial judge
Deference given to lower court	No deference	Substantial deference	Extreme deference
Party typically benefitted	Appellant	Appellee	Appellee
Definition	An appellate court reviews the legal question anew and independently, without regard to the conclusions reached by the trial court. "When *de novo* review is compelled, no form of appellate deference is acceptable." *Salve Regina College v. Russell,* (1991).	A finding is 'clearly erroneous' when although there is evidence to support it, the reviewing court on the entire evidence is left with the definite and firm conviction that a mistake has been committed. *United States v. United States Gypsum Co.,* (1948) "If the district court's account of the evidence is plausible in light of the record viewed in its entirety, the court of appeals may not reverse it even though convinced that had it been sitting as the trier of fact, it would have weighed the evidence differently. When there are two permissible views of the evidence, the factfinder's choice between them cannot be clearly erroneous." *Anderson v. Bessemer City,* (1985).	Generally, an abuse of discretion only occurs where no reasonable person could take the view adopted by the trial court. If reasonable persons could differ, no abuse of discretion can be found. *Harrington v. DeVito,* (7th Cir.1981) Under the abuse of discretion standard, a trial court's decision will not be disturbed unless the appellate court has a definite and firm conviction that the lower court made a clear error of judgment or exceeded the bounds of permissible choice in the circumstances. We will not alter a trial court's decision unless it can be shown that the court's decision was an arbitrary, capricious, whimsical, or manifestly unreasonable judgment. *Wright v. Abbott Laboratories, Inc.,* (10th Cir. 2001)
Examples	Motions for summary judgment, constitutional questions, statutory interpretation	Questions regarding who did what, where, and when; questions of intent and motive; questions of ultimate fact (such as negligence)	Rule 11 sanctions, attorney's fees, courtroom management, motions to compel, injunctions, and temporary restraining orders.

The Massachusetts Court System

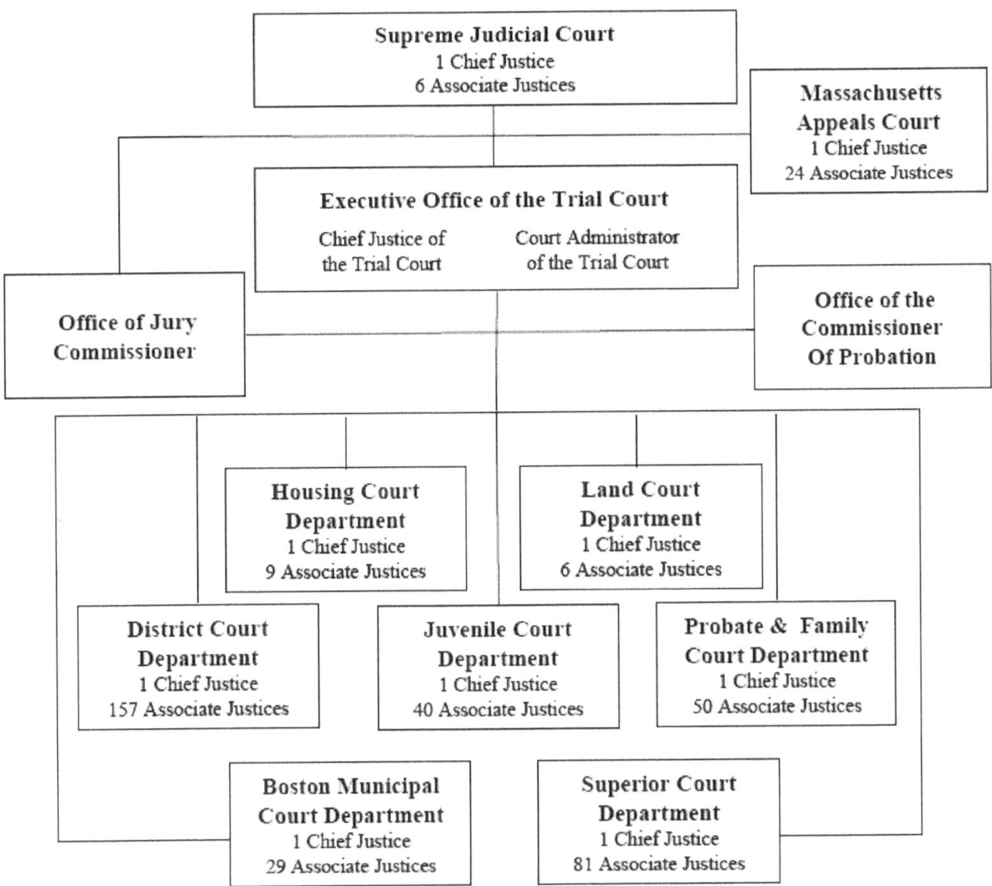

Notes for active learning

The Massachusetts Courts' Structure

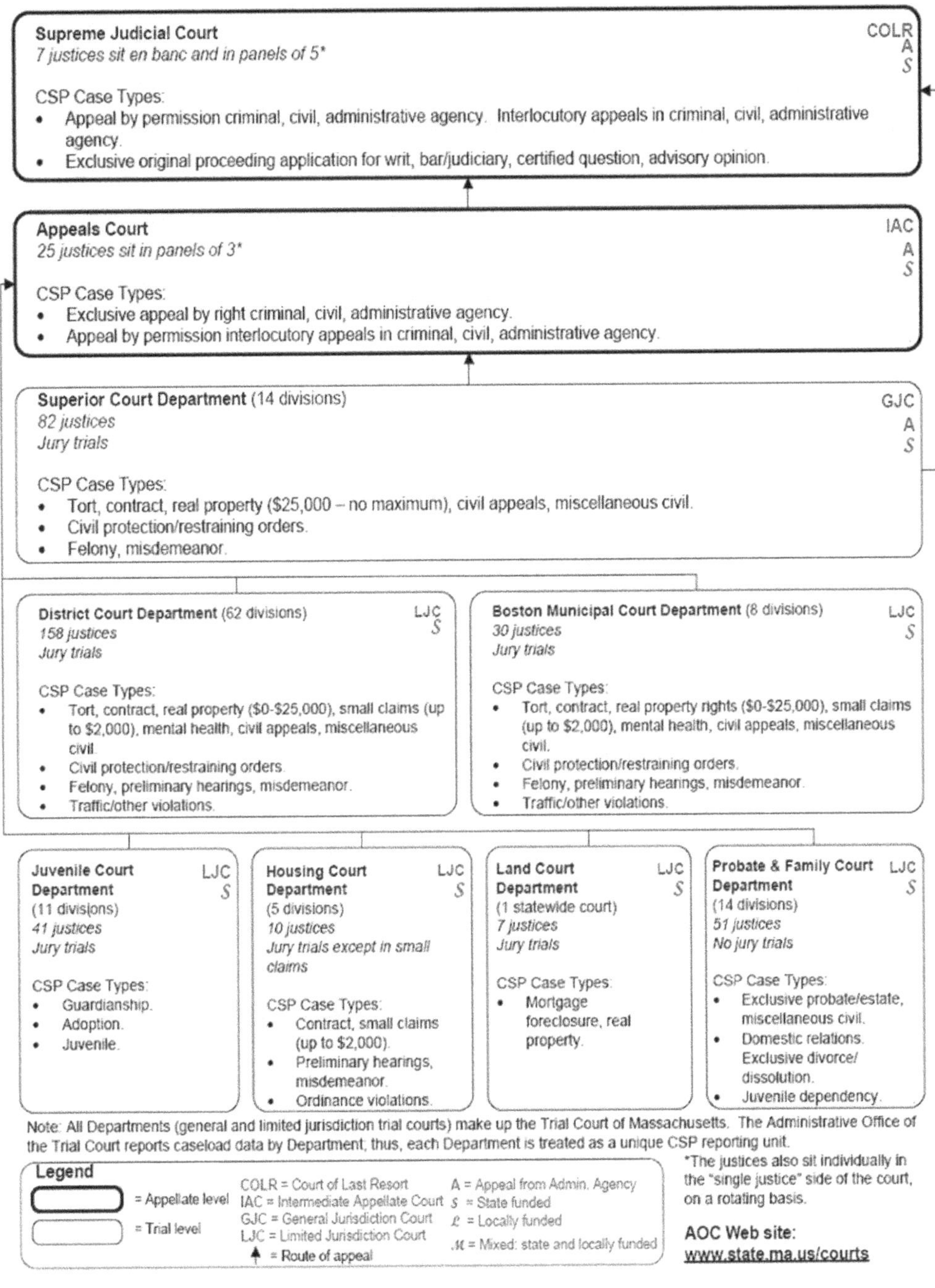

Notes for active learning

The New York Courts' Structure

Civil court structure

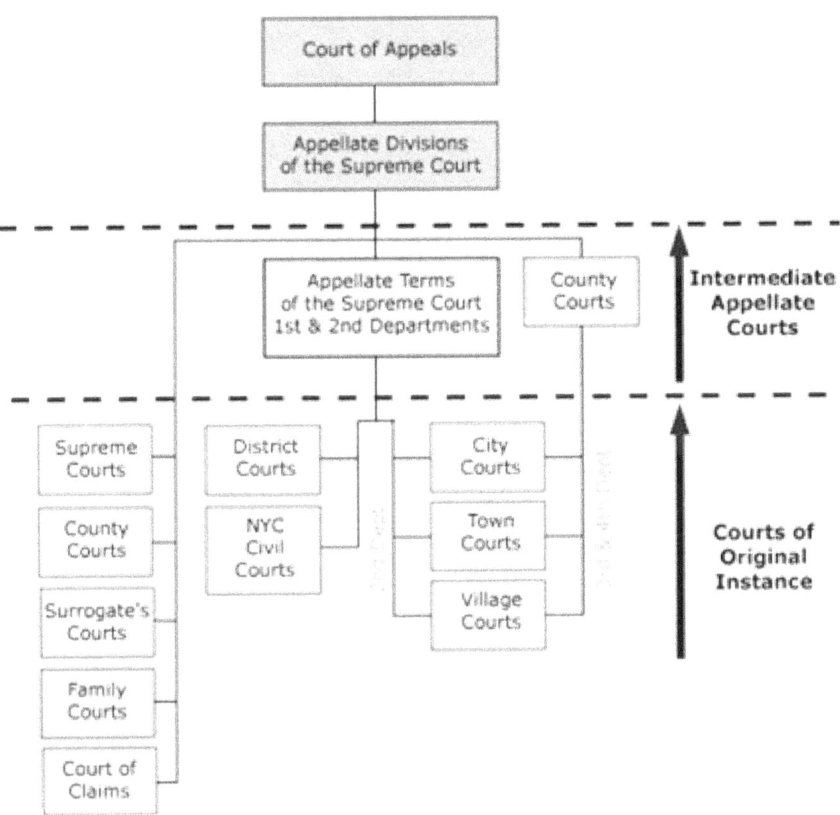

Criminal court structure

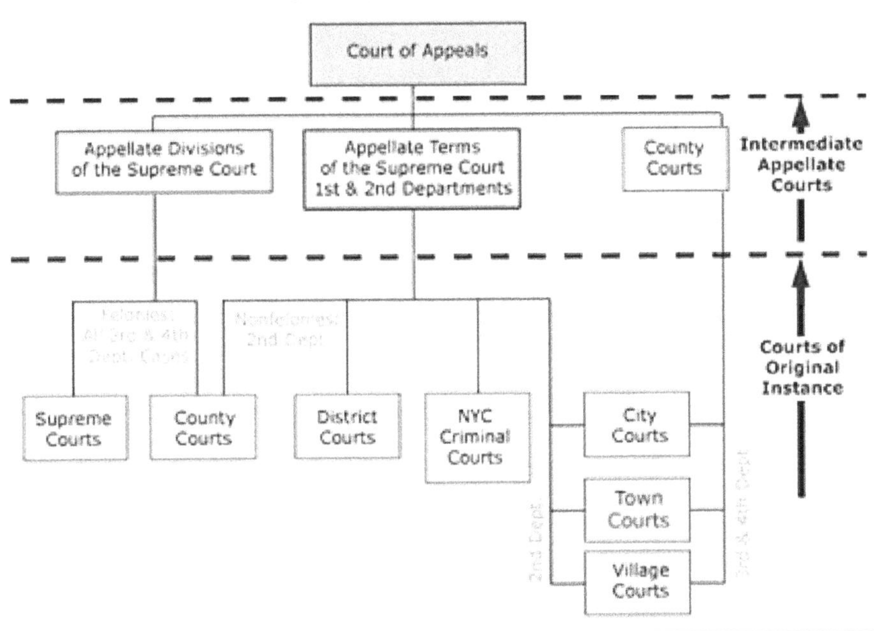

Notes for active learning

The Constitution of the United States (*a transcription*)

THE U.S. NATIONAL ARCHIVES & RECORDS ADMINISTRATION
www.archives.gov

The following text is a transcription of the Constitution as it was inscribed by Jacob Shallus on parchment (the document on display in the Rotunda at the National Archives Museum.) The spelling and punctuation reflect the original.

The Constitution of the United States: A Transcription

The following text is a transcription of the Constitution as it was inscribed by Jacob Shallus on parchment (displayed in the Rotunda at the National Archives Museum.) The authenticated text of the Constitution can be found on the website of the Government Printing Office.

We the People of the United States, in Order to form a more perfect Union, establish Justice, insure domestic Tranquility, provide for the common defence, promote the general Welfare, and secure the Blessings of Liberty to ourselves and our Posterity, do ordain and establish this Constitution for the United States of America.

Article. I

Section. 1.

All legislative Powers herein granted shall be vested in a Congress of the United States, which shall consist of a Senate and House of Representatives.

Section. 2.

The House of Representatives shall be composed of Members chosen every second Year by the People of the several States, and the Electors in each State shall have the Qualifications requisite for Electors of the most numerous Branch of the State Legislature.

No Person shall be a Representative who shall not have attained to the Age of twenty five Years, and been seven Years a Citizen of the United States, and who shall not, when elected, be an Inhabitant of that State in which he shall be chosen.

Representatives and direct Taxes shall be apportioned among the several States which may be included within this Union, according to their respective Numbers, which shall be determined by adding to the whole Number of free Persons, including those bound to Service for a Term of Years, and excluding Indians not taxed, three fifths of all other Persons. The actual Enumeration shall be made within three Years after the first Meeting of the Congress of the United States, and within every subsequent Term of ten Years, in such Manner as they shall by Law direct. The Number of Representatives shall not exceed one for every thirty Thousand, but each State shall have at Least one Representative; and until such enumeration shall be made, the State of New Hampshire shall be entitled to chuse three, Massachusetts eight, Rhode-Island and Providence

Plantations one, Connecticut five, New-York six, New Jersey four, Pennsylvania eight, Delaware one, Maryland six, Virginia ten, North Carolina five, South Carolina five, and Georgia three.

When vacancies happen in the Representation from any State, the Executive Authority thereof shall issue Writs of Election to fill such Vacancies.

The House of Representatives shall chuse their Speaker and other Officers; and shall have the sole Power of Impeachment.

Section. 3.

The Senate of the United States shall be composed of two Senators from each State, chosen by the Legislature thereof, for six Years; and each Senator shall have one Vote.

Immediately after they shall be assembled in Consequence of the first Election, they shall be divided as equally as may be into three Classes. The Seats of the Senators of the first Class shall be vacated at the Expiration of the second Year, of the second Class at the Expiration of the fourth Year, and of the third Class at the Expiration of the sixth Year, so that one third may be chosen every second Year; and if Vacancies happen by Resignation, or otherwise, during the Recess of the Legislature of any State, the Executive thereof may make temporary Appointments until the next Meeting of the Legislature, which shall then fill such Vacancies.

No Person shall be a Senator who shall not have attained to the Age of thirty Years, and been nine Years a Citizen of the United States, and who shall not, when elected, be an Inhabitant of that State for which he shall be chosen.

The Vice President of the United States shall be President of the Senate, but shall have no Vote, unless they be equally divided.

The Senate shall chuse their other Officers, and also a President pro tempore, in the Absence of the Vice President, or when he shall exercise the Office of President of the United States.

The Senate shall have the sole Power to try all Impeachments. When sitting for that Purpose, they shall be on Oath or Affirmation. When the President of the United States is tried, the Chief Justice shall preside: And no Person shall be convicted without the Concurrence of two thirds of the Members present.

Judgment in Cases of Impeachment shall not extend further than to removal from Office, and disqualification to hold and enjoy any Office of honor, Trust or Profit under the United States: but the Party convicted shall nevertheless be liable and subject to Indictment, Trial, Judgment and Punishment, according to Law.

Section. 4.

The Times, Places and Manner of holding Elections for Senators and Representatives, shall be prescribed in each State by the Legislature thereof; but the Congress may at any time by Law make or alter such Regulations, except as to the Places of chusing Senators.

The Congress shall assemble at least once in every Year, and such Meeting shall be on the first Monday in December, unless they shall by Law appoint a different Day.

Section. 5.

Each House shall be the Judge of the Elections, Returns and Qualifications of its own Members, and a Majority of each shall constitute a Quorum to do Business; but a smaller Number may adjourn from day to day, and may be authorized to compel the Attendance of absent Members, in such Manner, and under such Penalties as each House may provide.

Each House may determine the Rules of its Proceedings, punish its Members for disorderly Behaviour, and, with the Concurrence of two thirds, expel a Member.

Each House shall keep a Journal of its Proceedings, and from time to time publish the same, excepting such Parts as may in their Judgment require Secrecy; and the Yeas and Nays of the Members of either House on any question shall, at the Desire of one fifth of those Present, be entered on the Journal.

Neither House, during the Session of Congress, shall, without the Consent of the other, adjourn for more than three days, nor to any other Place than that in which the two Houses shall be sitting.

Section. 6.

The Senators and Representatives shall receive a Compensation for their Services, to be ascertained by Law, and paid out of the Treasury of the United States. They shall in all Cases, except Treason, Felony and Breach of the Peace, be privileged from Arrest during their Attendance at the Session of their respective Houses, and in going to and returning from the same; and for any Speech or Debate in either House, they shall not be questioned in any other Place.

No Senator or Representative shall, during the Time for which he was elected, be appointed to any civil Office under the Authority of the United States, which shall have been created, or the Emoluments whereof shall have been encreased during such time; and no Person holding any Office under the United States, shall be a Member of either House during his Continuance in Office.

Section. 7.

All Bills for raising Revenue shall originate in the House of Representatives; but the Senate may propose or concur with Amendments as on other Bills.

Every Bill which shall have passed the House of Representatives and the Senate, shall, before it become a Law, be presented to the President of the United States; If he approves he shall sign it, but if not he shall return it, with his Objections to that House in which it shall have originated, who shall enter the Objections at large on their Journal, and proceed to reconsider it. If after such Reconsideration two thirds of that House shall agree to pass the Bill, it shall be sent, together with the Objections, to the other House, by which it shall likewise be reconsidered, and if approved by two thirds of that House, it shall become a Law. But in all such Cases the Votes of both Houses shall be determined by yeas and Nays, and the Names of the Persons voting for and against the Bill shall be entered on the Journal of each House respectively. If any Bill shall not be returned by the President within ten Days (Sundays excepted) after it shall have been presented to him, the Same shall be a Law, in like Manner as if he had signed it, unless the Congress by their Adjournment prevent its Return, in which Case it shall not be a Law.

Every Order, Resolution, or Vote to which the Concurrence of the Senate and House of Representatives may be necessary (except on a question of Adjournment) shall be presented to the President of the United States; and before the Same shall take Effect, shall be approved by him, or being disapproved by him, shall be repassed by two thirds of the Senate and House of Representatives, according to the Rules and Limitations prescribed in the Case of a Bill.

Section. 8.

The Congress shall have Power To lay and collect Taxes, Duties, Imposts and Excises, to pay the Debts and provide for the common Defence and general Welfare of the United States; but all Duties, Imposts and Excises shall be uniform throughout the United States;

To borrow Money on the credit of the United States;

To regulate Commerce with foreign Nations, and among the several States, and with the Indian Tribes;

To establish an uniform Rule of Naturalization, and uniform Laws on the subject of Bankruptcies throughout the United States;

To coin Money, regulate the Value thereof, and of foreign Coin, and fix the Standard of Weights and Measures;

To provide for the Punishment of counterfeiting the Securities and current Coin of the United States;

To establish Post Offices and post Roads;

To promote the Progress of Science and useful Arts, by securing for limited Times to Authors and Inventors the exclusive Right to their respective Writings and Discoveries;

To constitute Tribunals inferior to the Supreme Court;

To define and punish Piracies and Felonies committed on the high Seas, and Offences against the Law of Nations;

To declare War, grant Letters of Marque and Reprisal, and make Rules concerning Captures on Land and Water;

To raise and support Armies, but no Appropriation of Money to that Use shall be for a longer Term than two Years;

To provide and maintain a Navy;

To make Rules for the Government and Regulation of the land and naval Forces;

To provide for calling forth the Militia to execute the Laws of the Union, suppress Insurrections and repel Invasions;

To provide for organizing, arming, and disciplining, the Militia, and for governing such Part of them as may be employed in the Service of the United States, reserving to the States respectively, the Appointment of the Officers, and the Authority of training the Militia according to the discipline prescribed by Congress;

To exercise exclusive Legislation in all Cases whatsoever, over such District (not exceeding ten Miles square) as may, by Cession of particular States, and the Acceptance of Congress, become the Seat of the Government of the United States, and to exercise like Authority over all Places purchased by the Consent of the Legislature of the State in which the Same shall be, for the Erection of Forts, Magazines, Arsenals, dock-Yards, and other needful Buildings;—And

To make all Laws which shall be necessary and proper for carrying into Execution the foregoing Powers, and all other Powers vested by this Constitution in the Government of the United States, or in any Department or Officer thereof.

Section. 9.

The Migration or Importation of such Persons as any of the States now existing shall think proper to admit, shall not be prohibited by the Congress prior to the Year one thousand eight hundred and eight, but a Tax or duty may be imposed on such Importation, not exceeding ten dollars for each Person.

The Privilege of the Writ of Habeas Corpus shall not be suspended, unless when in Cases of Rebellion or Invasion the public Safety may require it.

No Bill of Attainder or ex post facto Law shall be passed.

No Capitation, or other direct, Tax shall be laid, unless in Proportion to the Census or enumeration herein before directed to be taken.

No Tax or Duty shall be laid on Articles exported from any State.

No Preference shall be given by any Regulation of Commerce or Revenue to the Ports of one State over those of another: nor shall Vessels bound to, or from, one State, be obliged to enter, clear, or pay Duties in another.

No Money shall be drawn from the Treasury, but in Consequence of Appropriations made by Law; and a regular Statement and Account of the Receipts and Expenditures of all public Money shall be published from time to time.

No Title of Nobility shall be granted by the United States: And no Person holding any Office of Profit or Trust under them, shall, without the Consent of the Congress, accept of any present, Emolument, Office, or Title, of any kind whatever, from any King, Prince, or foreign State.

Section. 10.

No State shall enter into any Treaty, Alliance, or Confederation; grant Letters of Marque and Reprisal; coin Money; emit Bills of Credit; make any Thing but gold and silver Coin a Tender in Payment of Debts; pass any Bill of Attainder, ex post facto Law, or Law impairing the Obligation of Contracts, or grant any Title of Nobility.

No State shall, without the Consent of the Congress, lay any Imposts or Duties on Imports or Exports, except what may be absolutely necessary for executing it's inspection Laws: and the net

Produce of all Duties and Imposts, laid by any State on Imports or Exports, shall be for the Use of the Treasury of the United States; and all such Laws shall be subject to the Revision and Controul of the Congress.

No State shall, without the Consent of Congress, lay any Duty of Tonnage, keep Troops, or Ships of War in time of Peace, enter into any Agreement or Compact with another State, or with a foreign Power, or engage in War, unless actually invaded, or in such imminent Danger as will not admit of delay.

Article. II

Section. 1.

The executive Power shall be vested in a President of the United States of America. He shall hold his Office during the Term of four Years, and, together with the Vice President, chosen for the same Term, be elected, as follows

Each State shall appoint, in such Manner as the Legislature thereof may direct, a Number of Electors, equal to the whole Number of Senators and Representatives to which the State may be entitled in the Congress: but no Senator or Representative, or Person holding an Office of Trust or Profit under the United States, shall be appointed an Elector.

The Electors shall meet in their respective States, and vote by Ballot for two Persons, of whom one at least shall not be an Inhabitant of the same State with themselves. And they shall make a List of all the Persons voted for, and of the Number of Votes for each; which List they shall sign and certify, and transmit sealed to the Seat of the Government of the United States, directed to the President of the Senate. The President of the Senate shall, in the Presence of the Senate and House of Representatives, open all the Certificates, and the Votes shall then be counted. The Person having the greatest Number of Votes shall be the President, if such Number be a Majority of the whole Number of Electors appointed; and if there be more than one who have such Majority, and have an equal Number of Votes, then the House of Representatives shall immediately chuse by Ballot one of them for President; and if no Person have a Majority, then from the five highest on the List the said House shall in like Manner chuse the President. But in chusing the President, the Votes shall be taken by States, the Representation from each State having one Vote; A quorum for this Purpose shall consist of a Member or Members from two thirds of the States, and a Majority of all the States shall be necessary to a Choice. In every Case, after the Choice of the President, the Person having the greatest Number of Votes of the Electors shall be the Vice President. But if there should remain two or more who have equal Votes, the Senate shall chuse from them by Ballot the Vice President.

The Congress may determine the Time of chusing the Electors, and the Day on which they shall give their Votes; which Day shall be the same throughout the United States.

No Person except a natural born Citizen, or a Citizen of the United States, at the time of the Adoption of this Constitution, shall be eligible to the Office of President; neither shall any Person be eligible to that Office who shall not have attained to the Age of thirty five Years, and been fourteen Years a Resident within the United States.

In Case of the Removal of the President from Office, or of his Death, Resignation, or Inability to discharge the Powers and Duties of the said Office, the Same shall devolve on the Vice President, and the Congress may by Law provide for the Case of Removal, Death, Resignation or Inability, both of the President and Vice President, declaring what Officer shall then act as President, and such Officer shall act accordingly, until the Disability be removed, or a President shall be elected.

The President shall, at stated Times, receive for his Services, a Compensation, which shall neither be encreased nor diminished during the Period for which he shall have been elected, and he shall not receive within that Period any other Emolument from the United States, or any of them.

Before he enters on the Execution of his Office, he shall take the following Oath or Affirmation:—"I do solemnly swear (or affirm) that I will faithfully execute the Office of President of the United States, and will to the best of my Ability, preserve, protect and defend the Constitution of the United States."

Section. 2.

The President shall be Commander in Chief of the Army and Navy of the United States, and of the Militia of the several States, when called into the actual Service of the United States; he may require the Opinion, in writing, of the principal Officer in each of the executive Departments, upon any Subject relating to the Duties of their respective Offices, and he shall have Power to grant Reprieves and Pardons for Offences against the United States, except in Cases of Impeachment.

He shall have Power, by and with the Advice and Consent of the Senate, to make Treaties, provided two thirds of the Senators present concur; and he shall nominate, and by and with the Advice and Consent of the Senate, shall appoint Ambassadors, other public Ministers and Consuls, Judges of the supreme Court, and all other Officers of the United States, whose Appointments are not herein otherwise provided for, and which shall be established by Law: but the Congress may by Law vest the Appointment of such inferior Officers, as they think proper, in the President alone, in the Courts of Law, or in the Heads of Departments.

The President shall have Power to fill up all Vacancies that may happen during the Recess of the Senate, by granting Commissions which shall expire at the End of their next Session.

Section. 3.

He shall from time to time give to the Congress Information of the State of the Union, and recommend to their Consideration such Measures as he shall judge necessary and expedient; he may, on extraordinary Occasions, convene both Houses, or either of them, and in Case of Disagreement between them, with Respect to the Time of Adjournment, he may adjourn them to such Time as he shall think proper; he shall receive Ambassadors and other public Ministers; he shall take Care that the Laws be faithfully executed, and shall Commission all the Officers of the United States.

Section. 4.

The President, Vice President and all civil Officers of the United States, shall be removed from Office on Impeachment for, and Conviction of, Treason, Bribery, or other high Crimes and Misdemeanors.

Article III

Section. 1.

The judicial Power of the United States, shall be vested in one supreme Court, and in such inferior Courts as the Congress may from time to time ordain and establish. The Judges, both of the supreme and inferior Courts, shall hold their Offices during good Behaviour, and shall, at stated Times, receive for their Services, a Compensation, which shall not be diminished during their Continuance in Office.

Section. 2.

The judicial Power shall extend to all Cases, in Law and Equity, arising under this Constitution, the Laws of the United States, and Treaties made, or which shall be made, under their Authority;—to all Cases affecting Ambassadors, other public Ministers and Consuls;—to all Cases of admiralty and maritime Jurisdiction;—to Controversies to which the United States shall be a Party;—to Controversies between two or more States;—between a State and Citizens of another State,—between Citizens of different States,—between Citizens of the same State claiming Lands under Grants of different States, and between a State, or the Citizens thereof, and foreign States, Citizens or Subjects.

In all Cases affecting Ambassadors, other public Ministers and Consuls, and those in which a State shall be Party, the supreme Court shall have original Jurisdiction. In all the other Cases before mentioned, the supreme Court shall have appellate Jurisdiction, both as to Law and Fact, with such Exceptions, and under such Regulations as the Congress shall make.

The Trial of all Crimes, except in Cases of Impeachment, shall be by Jury; and such Trial shall be held in the State where the said Crimes shall have been committed; but when not committed within any State, the Trial shall be at such Place or Places as the Congress may by Law have directed.

Section. 3.

Treason against the United States, shall consist only in levying War against them, or in adhering to their Enemies, giving them Aid and Comfort. No Person shall be convicted of Treason unless on the Testimony of two Witnesses to the same overt Act, or on Confession in open Court.

The Congress shall have Power to declare the Punishment of Treason, but no Attainder of Treason shall work Corruption of Blood, or Forfeiture except during the Life of the Person attainted.

Article. IV

Section. 1.

Full Faith and Credit shall be given in each State to the public Acts, Records, and judicial Proceedings of every other State. And the Congress may by general Laws prescribe the Manner in which such Acts, Records and Proceedings shall be proved, and the Effect thereof.

Section. 2.

The Citizens of each State shall be entitled to all Privileges and Immunities of Citizens in the several States.

A Person charged in any State with Treason, Felony, or other Crime, who shall flee from Justice, and be found in another State, shall on Demand of the executive Authority of the State from which he fled, be delivered up, to be removed to the State having Jurisdiction of the Crime.

No Person held to Service or Labour in one State, under the Laws thereof, escaping into another, shall, in Consequence of any Law or Regulation therein, be discharged from such Service or Labour, but shall be delivered up on Claim of the Party to whom such Service or Labour may be due.

Section. 3.

New States may be admitted by the Congress into this Union; but no new State shall be formed or erected within the Jurisdiction of any other State; nor any State be formed by the Junction of two or more States, or Parts of States, without the Consent of the Legislatures of the States concerned as well as of the Congress.

The Congress shall have Power to dispose of and make all needful Rules and Regulations respecting the Territory or other Property belonging to the United States; and nothing in this Constitution shall be so construed as to Prejudice any Claims of the United States, or of any particular State.

Section. 4.

The United States shall guarantee to every State in this Union a Republican Form of Government, and shall protect each of them against Invasion; and on Application of the Legislature, or of the Executive (when the Legislature cannot be convened), against domestic Violence.

Article. V

The Congress, whenever two thirds of both Houses shall deem it necessary, shall propose Amendments to this Constitution, or, on the Application of the Legislatures of two thirds of the several States, shall call a Convention for proposing Amendments, which, in either Case, shall be valid to all Intents and Purposes, as Part of this Constitution, when ratified by the Legislatures of three fourths of the several States, or by Conventions in three fourths thereof, as the one or the other Mode of Ratification may be proposed by the Congress; Provided that no Amendment which may be made prior to the Year One thousand eight hundred and eight shall in any Manner affect the first and fourth Clauses in the Ninth Section of the first Article; and that no State, without its Consent, shall be deprived of its equal Suffrage in the Senate.

Article. VI

All Debts contracted and Engagements entered into, before the Adoption of this Constitution, shall be as valid against the United States under this Constitution, as under the Confederation.

This Constitution, and the Laws of the United States which shall be made in Pursuance thereof; and all Treaties made, or which shall be made, under the Authority of the United States, shall be the supreme Law of the Land; and the Judges in every State shall be bound thereby, any Thing in the Constitution or Laws of any State to the Contrary notwithstanding.

The Senators and Representatives before mentioned, and the Members of the several State Legislatures, and all executive and judicial Officers, both of the United States and of the several States, shall be bound by Oath or Affirmation, to support this Constitution; but no religious Test shall ever be required as a Qualification to any Office or public Trust under the United States.

Article. VII

The Ratification of the Conventions of nine States, shall be sufficient for the Establishment of this Constitution between the States so ratifying the Same.

The Word, "the," being interlined between the seventh and eighth Lines of the first Page, The Word "Thirty" being partly written on an Erazure in the fifteenth Line of the first Page, The Words "is tried" being interlined between the thirty second and thirty third Lines of the first Page and the Word "the" being interlined between the forty third and forty fourth Lines of the second Page.

Attest William Jackson Secretary, done in Convention by the Unanimous Consent of the States present the Seventeenth Day of September in the Year of our Lord one thousand seven hundred and Eighty seven and of the Independance of the United States of America the Twelfth In witness whereof We have hereunto subscribed our Names, G°. Washington, *Presidt and deputy from Virginia*

Delaware
Geo: Read
Gunning Bedford jun
John Dickinson
Richard Bassett
Jaco: Broom

Maryland
James McHenry
Dan of St Thos.
Jenifer
Danl. Carroll

Virginia
John Blair
James Madison Jr.

North Carolina
Wm. Blount
Richd. Dobbs
Spaight
Hu Williamson

South Carolina
J. Rutledge
Charles Cotesworth
Pinckney
Charles Pinckney
Pierce Butler

Georgia
William Few
Abr Baldwin

New Hampshire
John Langdon
Nicholas Gilman

Massachusetts
Nathaniel Gorham
Rufus King

Connecticut
Wm. Saml. Johnson
Roger Sherman

New York
Alexander Hamilton

New Jersey
Wil: Livingston
David Brearley
Wm. Paterson
Jona: Dayton

Pensylvania
B Franklin
Thomas Mifflin
Robt. Morris
Geo. Clymer
Thos. FitzSimons
Jared Ingersoll
James Wilson
Gouv Morris

Enactment of the Bill of Rights of the United States of America (1791)

The first ten Amendments to the Constitution make up the Bill of Rights. Written by James Madison in response to calls from several states for greater constitutional protection for individual liberties, the Bill of Rights lists specific prohibitions on governmental power. The Virginia Declaration of Rights, written by George Mason, strongly influenced Madison.

One of the contention points between Federalists and Anti-Federalists was the Constitution's lack of a bill of rights that would place specific limits on government power.

Federalists argued that the Constitution did not need a bill of rights because the people and the states kept powers not explicitly given to the federal government.

Anti-Federalists held that a *bill of rights* was necessary to safeguard individual liberty.

Madison, then a member of the U.S. House of Representatives, went through the Constitution itself, making changes where he thought most appropriate.

Several Representatives, led by Roger Sherman, objected that Congress had no authority to change the wording of the Constitution. Therefore, Madison's changes were presented as a list of amendments that would follow Article VII.

The House approved 17 amendments. Of these 17, the Senate approved 12. Those 12 were sent to the states for approval in August of 1789. Of those 12 proposed amendments, 10 were quickly ratified. Virginia's legislature became the last to ratify the Amendments on December 15, 1791. These Amendments are the Bill of Rights.

The Bill of Rights is a list of limits on government power. For example, what the Founders saw as the natural right of individuals to speak and worship freely was protected by the First Amendment's prohibitions on Congress from making laws establishing a religion or abridging freedom of speech.

Another example is the natural right to be free from the government's unreasonable intrusion in one's home was safeguarded by the Fourth Amendment's warrant requirements.

Other precursors to the Bill of Rights include English documents such as the Magna Carta[1], the Petition of Rights, the English Bill of Rights, and the Massachusetts Body of Liberties.

The Magna Carta illustrates Compact Theory[1] as well as initial strides toward limited government. Its provisions address individual rights and political rights. Latin for "Great Charter," the Magna Carta was written by Barons in Runnymede, England, and forced on the King.

Although the protections were generally limited to the prerogatives of the Barons, the Magna Carta embodied the general principle that the King accepted limitations on his rule. These included the fundamental acknowledgment that the king was not above the law.

Included in the Magna Carta are protections for the English church, petitioning the king, freedom from the forced quarter of troops and unreasonable searches, due process and fair trial protections, and freedom from excessive fines. These protections can be found in the First, Third, Fourth, Fifth, Sixth, and Eighth Amendments to the Constitution.

The Magna Carta is the oldest compact in England. The Mayflower Compact, the Fundamental Orders of Connecticut, and the Albany Plan are examples from the American colonies.

The Articles of Confederation was a compact among the states, and the Constitution creates a compact based on a federal system between the national government, state governments, and the people. The Hayne-Webster Debate focused on the compact created by the Constitution.

[1] Philosophers including Thomas Hobbes, John Locke, and Jean-Jacques Rousseau theorized that peoples' condition in a "state of nature" (that is, outside of society) is one of freedom, but that freedom inevitably degrades into war, chaos, or debilitating competition without the benefit of a system of laws and government. They reasoned, therefore, that for their happiness, individuals willingly trade some of their natural freedom in exchange for the protections provided by the government.

The Bill of Rights: Amendments I–X

Amendment I

Congress shall make no law respecting an establishment of religion, or prohibiting the free exercise thereof; or abridging the freedom of speech, or of the press; or the right of the people peaceably to assemble, and to petition the government for a redress of grievances.

Amendment II

A well regulated militia, being necessary to the security of a free state, the right of the people to keep and bear arms, shall not be infringed.

Amendment III

No soldier shall, in time of peace be quartered in any house, without the consent of the owner, nor in time of war, but in a manner to be prescribed by law.

Amendment IV

The right of the people to be secure in their persons, houses, papers, and effects, against unreasonable searches and seizures, shall not be violated, and no warrants shall issue, but upon probable cause, supported by oath or affirmation, and particularly describing the place to be searched, and the persons or things to be seized.

Amendment V

No person shall be held to answer for a capital, or otherwise infamous crime, unless on a presentment or indictment of a grand jury, except in cases arising in the land or naval forces, or in the militia, when in actual service in time of war or public danger; nor shall any person be subject for the same offense to be twice put in jeopardy of life or limb; nor shall be compelled in any criminal case to be a witness against himself, nor be deprived of life, liberty, or property, without due process of law; nor shall private property be taken for public use, without just compensation.

Amendment VI

In all criminal prosecutions, the accused shall enjoy the right to a speedy and public trial, by an impartial jury of the state and district wherein the crime shall have been committed, which district shall have been previously ascertained by law, and to be informed of the nature and cause of the accusation; to be confronted with the witnesses against him; to have compulsory process for obtaining witnesses in his favor, and to have the assistance of counsel for his defense.

Amendment VII

In suits at common law, where the value in controversy shall exceed twenty dollars, the right of trial by jury shall be preserved, and no fact tried by a jury, shall be otherwise reexamined in any court of the United States, than according to the rules of the common law.

Amendment VIII

Excessive bail shall not be required, nor excessive fines imposed, nor cruel and unusual punishments inflicted.

Amendment IX

The enumeration in the Constitution, of certain rights, shall not be construed to deny or disparage others retained by the people.

Amendment X

The powers not delegated to the United States by the Constitution, nor prohibited by it to the states, are reserved to the states respectively, or to the people.

Constitutional Amendments XI–XXVII

AMENDMENT XI

Passed by Congress March 4, 1794. Ratified February 7, 1795.

Note: Article III, section 2, of the Constitution was modified by amendment 11.

The Judicial power of the United States shall not be construed to extend to any suit in law or equity, commenced or prosecuted against one of the United States by Citizens of another State, or by Citizens or Subjects of any Foreign State.

AMENDMENT XII

Passed by Congress December 9, 1803. Ratified June 15, 1804.

Note: A portion of Article II, section 1 of the Constitution was superseded by the 12th amendment.

The Electors shall meet in their respective states and vote by ballot for President and Vice-President, one of whom, at least, shall not be an inhabitant of the same state with themselves; they shall name in their ballots the person voted for as President, and in distinct ballots the person voted for as Vice-President, and they shall make distinct lists of all persons voted for as President, and of all persons voted for as Vice-President, and of the number of votes for each, which lists they shall sign and certify, and transmit sealed to the seat of the government of the United States, directed to the President of the Senate; -- the President of the Senate shall, in the presence of the Senate and House of Representatives, open all the certificates and the votes shall then be counted; -- The person having the greatest number of votes for President, shall be the President, if such number be a majority of the whole number of Electors appointed; and if no person have such majority, then from the persons having the highest numbers not exceeding three on the list of those voted for as President, the House of Representatives shall choose immediately, by ballot, the President. But in choosing the President, the votes shall be taken by states, the representation from each state having one vote; a quorum for this purpose shall consist of a member or members from two-thirds of the states, and a majority of all the states shall be necessary to a choice. [And if the House of Representatives shall not choose a President whenever the right of choice shall devolve upon them, before the fourth day of March next following, then the Vice-President shall act as President, as in case of the death or other constitutional disability of the President. --]* The person having the greatest number of votes as Vice-President, shall be the Vice-President, if such number be a majority of the whole number of Electors appointed, and if no person have a majority, then from the two highest numbers on the list, the Senate shall choose the Vice-President; a quorum for the purpose shall consist of two-thirds of the whole number of Senators, and a majority of the whole number shall be necessary to a choice. But no person constitutionally ineligible to the office of President shall be eligible to that of Vice-President of the United States.

**Superseded by section 3 of the 20th Amendment.*

AMENDMENT XIII

Passed by Congress January 31, 1865. Ratified December 6, 1865.

Note: A portion of Article IV, section 2, of the Constitution was superseded by the 13th amendment.

Section 1.

Neither slavery nor involuntary servitude, except as a punishment for crime whereof the party shall have been duly convicted, shall exist within the United States, or any place subject to their jurisdiction.

Section 2.

Congress shall have power to enforce this article by appropriate legislation.

AMENDMENT XIV

Passed by Congress June 13, 1866. Ratified July 9, 1868.

Note: Article I, section 2, of the Constitution was modified by section 2 of the 14th amendment.

Section 1.

All persons born or naturalized in the United States, and subject to the jurisdiction thereof, are citizens of the United States and of the State wherein they reside. No State shall make or enforce any law which shall abridge the privileges or immunities of citizens of the United States; nor shall any State deprive any person of life, liberty, or property, without due process of law; nor deny to any person within its jurisdiction the equal protection of the laws.

Section 2.

Representatives shall be apportioned among the several States according to their respective numbers, counting the whole number of persons in each State, excluding Indians not taxed. But when the right to vote at any election for the choice of electors for President and Vice-President of the United States, Representatives in Congress, the Executive and Judicial officers of a State, or the members of the Legislature thereof, is denied to any of the male inhabitants of such State, being twenty-one years of age,* and citizens of the United States, or in any way abridged, except for participation in rebellion, or other crime, the basis of representation therein shall be reduced in the proportion which the number of such male citizens shall bear to the whole number of male citizens twenty-one years of age in such State.

Section 3.

No person shall be a Senator or Representative in Congress, or elector of President and Vice-President, or hold any office, civil or military, under the United States, or under any State, who, having previously taken an oath, as a member of Congress, or as an officer of the United States, or as a member of any State legislature, or as an executive or judicial officer of any State, to support the Constitution of the United States, shall have engaged in insurrection or rebellion against the same, or given aid or comfort to the enemies thereof. But Congress may by a vote of two-thirds of each House, remove such disability.

Section 4.

The validity of the public debt of the United States, authorized by law, including debts incurred for payment of pensions and bounties for services in suppressing insurrection or rebellion, shall not be questioned. But neither the United States nor any State shall assume or pay any debt or obligation incurred in aid of insurrection or rebellion against the United States, or any claim for the loss or emancipation of any slave; but all such debts, obligations and claims shall be held illegal and void.

Section 5.

The Congress shall have the power to enforce, by appropriate legislation, the provisions of this article.

**Changed by section 1 of the 26th Amendment.*

AMENDMENT XV

Passed by Congress February 26, 1869. Ratified February 3, 1870.

Section 1.

The right of citizens of the United States to vote shall not be denied or abridged by the United States or by any State on account of race, color, or previous condition of servitude.

Section 2.

The Congress shall have the power to enforce this article by appropriate legislation.

AMENDMENT XVI

Passed by Congress July 2, 1909. Ratified February 3, 1913.

Note: Article I, section 9, of the Constitution was modified by amendment 16.

The Congress shall have power to lay and collect taxes on incomes, from whatever source derived, without apportionment among the several States, and without regard to any census or enumeration.

AMENDMENT XVII

Passed by Congress May 13, 1912. Ratified April 8, 1913.

Note: Article I, section 3, of the Constitution was modified by the 17th Amendment.

The Senate of the United States shall be composed of two Senators from each State, elected by the people thereof, for six years; and each Senator shall have one vote. The electors in each State shall have the qualifications requisite for electors of the most numerous branch of the State legislatures.

When vacancies happen in the representation of any State in the Senate, the executive authority of such State shall issue writs of election to fill such vacancies: *Provided*, That the legislature of any State may empower the executive thereof to make temporary appointments until the people fill the vacancies by election as the legislature may direct.

This amendment shall not be so construed as to affect the election or term of any Senator chosen before it becomes valid as part of the Constitution.

AMENDMENT XVIII

Passed by Congress December 18, 1917. Ratified January 16, 1919. Repealed by Amendment 21.

Section 1.

After one year from the ratification of this article the manufacture, sale, or transportation of intoxicating liquors within, the importation thereof into, or the exportation thereof from the United States and all territory subject to the jurisdiction thereof for beverage purposes is hereby prohibited.

Section 2.

The Congress and the several States shall have concurrent power to enforce this article by appropriate legislation.

Section 3.

This article shall be inoperative unless it shall have been ratified as an amendment to the Constitution by the legislatures of the several States, as provided in the Constitution, within seven years from the date of the submission hereof to the States by the Congress.

AMENDMENT XIX

Passed by Congress June 4, 1919. Ratified August 18, 1920.

The right of citizens of the United States to vote shall not be denied or abridged by the United States or by any State on account of sex.

Congress shall have power to enforce this article by appropriate legislation.

AMENDMENT XX

Passed by Congress March 2, 1932. Ratified January 23, 1933.

Note: Article I, section 4, of the Constitution was modified by section 2 of this Amendment. In addition, a portion of the 12th Amendment was superseded by section 3.

Section 1.

The terms of the President and the Vice President shall end at noon on the 20th day of January, and the terms of Senators and Representatives at noon on the 3d day of January, of the years in which such terms would have ended if this article had not been ratified; and the terms of their successors shall then begin.

Section 2.

The Congress shall assemble at least once in every year, and such meeting shall begin at noon on the 3d day of January, unless they shall by law appoint a different day.

Section 3.

If, at the time fixed for the beginning of the term of the President, the President elect shall have died, the Vice President elect shall become President. If a President shall not have been chosen before the time fixed for the beginning of his term, or if the President elect shall have failed to qualify, then the Vice President elect shall act as President until a President shall have qualified; and the Congress may by law provide for the case wherein neither a President elect nor a Vice President elect shall have qualified, declaring who shall then act as President, or the manner in which one who is to act shall be selected, and such person shall act accordingly until a President or Vice President shall have qualified.

Section 4.

The Congress may by law provide for the case of the death of any of the persons from whom the House of Representatives may choose a President whenever the right of choice shall have devolved upon them, and for the case of the death of any of the persons from whom the Senate may choose a Vice President whenever the right of choice shall have devolved upon them.

Section 5.

Sections 1 and 2 shall take effect on the 15th day of October following the ratification of this article.

Section 6.

This article shall be inoperative unless it shall have been ratified as an amendment to the Constitution by the legislatures of three-fourths of the several States within seven years from the date of its submission.

AMENDMENT XXI

Passed by Congress February 20, 1933. Ratified December 5, 1933.

Section 1.

The eighteenth article of amendment to the Constitution of the United States is hereby repealed.

Section 2.

The transportation or importation into any State, Territory, or possession of the United States for delivery or use therein of intoxicating liquors, in violation of the laws thereof, is hereby prohibited.

Section 3.

This article shall be inoperative unless it shall have been ratified as an amendment to the Constitution by conventions in the several States, as provided in the Constitution, within seven years from the date of the submission hereof to the States by the Congress.

AMENDMENT XXII

Passed by Congress March 21, 1947. Ratified February 27, 1951.

Section 1.

No person shall be elected to the office of the President more than twice, and no person who has held the office of President, or acted as President, for more than two years of a term to which some other person was elected President shall be elected to the office of the President more than once. But this Article shall not apply to any person holding the office of President when this Article was proposed by the Congress, and shall not prevent any person who may be holding the office of President, or acting as President, during the term within which this Article becomes operative from holding the office of President or acting as President during the remainder of such term.

Section 2.

This article shall be inoperative unless it shall have been ratified as an amendment to the Constitution by the legislatures of three-fourths of the several States within seven years from the date of its submission to the States by the Congress.

AMENDMENT XXIII

Passed by Congress June 16, 1960. Ratified March 29, 1961.

Section 1.

The District constituting the seat of Government of the United States shall appoint in such manner as the Congress may direct:

A number of electors of President and Vice President equal to the whole number of Senators and Representatives in Congress to which the District would be entitled if it were a State, but in no event more than the least populous State; they shall be in addition to those appointed by the States, but they shall be considered, for the purposes of the election of President and Vice President, to be electors appointed by a State; and they shall meet in the District and perform such duties as provided by the twelfth article of amendment.

Section 2.

The Congress shall have power to enforce this article by appropriate legislation.

AMENDMENT XXIV

Passed by Congress August 27, 1962. Ratified January 23, 1964.

Section 1.

The right of citizens of the United States to vote in any primary or other election for President or Vice President, for electors for President or Vice President, or for Senator or Representative in Congress, shall not be denied or abridged by the United States or any State by reason of failure to pay any poll tax or other tax.

Section 2.

The Congress shall have power to enforce this article by appropriate legislation.

AMENDMENT XXV

Passed by Congress July 6, 1965. Ratified February 10, 1967.

Note: Article II, section 1, of the Constitution was affected by the 25th amendment.

Section 1.

In case of the removal of the President from office or of his death or resignation, the Vice President shall become President.

Section 2.

Whenever there is a vacancy in the office of the Vice President, the President shall nominate a Vice President who shall take office upon confirmation by a majority vote of both Houses of Congress.

Section 3.

Whenever the President transmits to the President pro tempore of the Senate and the Speaker of the House of Representatives his written declaration that he is unable to discharge the powers and duties of his office, and until he transmits to them a written declaration to the contrary, such powers and duties shall be discharged by the Vice President as Acting President.

Section 4.

Whenever the Vice President and a majority of either the principal officers of the executive departments or of such other body as Congress may by law provide, transmit to the President pro tempore of the Senate and the Speaker of the House of Representatives their written declaration that the President is unable to discharge the powers and duties of his office, the Vice President shall immediately assume the powers and duties of the office as Acting President.

Thereafter, when the President transmits to the President pro tempore of the Senate and the Speaker of the House of Representatives his written declaration that no inability exists, he shall resume the powers and duties of his office unless the Vice President and a majority of either the principal officers of the executive department or of such other body as Congress may by law provide, transmit within four days to the President pro tempore of the Senate and the Speaker of the House of Representatives their written declaration that the President is unable to discharge the powers and duties of his office. Thereupon Congress shall decide the issue, assembling within forty-eight hours for that purpose if not in session. If the Congress, within twenty-one days after receipt of the latter written declaration, or, if Congress is not in session, within twenty-one days after Congress is required to assemble, determines by two-thirds vote of both Houses that the President is unable to discharge the powers and duties of his office, the Vice President shall continue to discharge the same as Acting President; otherwise, the President shall resume the powers and duties of his office.

AMENDMENT XXVI

Passed by Congress March 23, 1971. Ratified July 1, 1971.

Note: Amendment 14, section 2, of the Constitution was modified by section 1 of the 26th amendment.

Section 1.

The right of citizens of the United States, who are eighteen years of age or older, to vote shall not be denied or abridged by the United States or by any State on account of age.

Section 2.

The Congress shall have power to enforce this article by appropriate legislation.

AMENDMENT XXVII

Originally proposed Sept. 25, 1789. Ratified May 7, 1992.

No law, varying the compensation for the services of the Senators and Representatives, shall take effect, until an election of Representatives shall have intervened

States' Rights Under the U.S. Constitution

Selective incorporation under the 14th Amendment

The U.S. Constitution has Articles and Amendments that established constitutional rights.

The provisions in the Bill of Rights (i.e., the first ten Amendments to the Constitution) were initially binding upon only the federal government.

In time, most of these provisions became binding upon the states through *selective incorporation* into the *due process clause* of the 14th Amendment (i.e., reverse incorporation).

When a provision is made binding on a state, a state can no longer restrict the rights guaranteed in that provision.

The 1st Amendment guarantees the freedoms of speech, press, religion, and assembly.

The 5th Amendment protects the right to grand jury proceedings in federal criminal cases.

The 6th Amendment guarantees a right to confront witnesses (i.e., Confrontation Clause).

The right to confront witnesses was not *selectively incorporated* into the due process clause of the 14th Amendment and is not binding upon the states.

Therefore, persons involved in state criminal proceedings as a defendant have no federal constitutional right to grand jury proceedings.

Whether an individual has a right to a grand jury becomes a question of state law.

The 10th Amendment, which is part of the **Bill of Rights**, was ratified on December 15, 1791. It states the Constitution's principle of **federalism** by providing that powers not granted to the **federal government** by the Constitution, nor prohibited to the **States**, are reserved to the States or the people.

Federalism in the United States

Federalism in the United States is the evolving relationship between **state governments** and the **federal government**.

The American government has evolved from a system of dual federalism to associative federalism.

In "Federalist No. 46," James Madison wrote that the states and national government "are in fact but different agents and trustees of the people, constituted with different powers."

Alexander Hamilton, in "Federalist No. 28," suggested that both levels of government would exercise authority to the citizens' benefit: "If their [the peoples'] rights are invaded by either, they can make use of the other as the instrument of redress."[3]

Because the states were preexisting political entities, the U.S. Constitution did not need to define or explain federalism in one section, but it often mentions the rights and responsibilities of state governments and state officials in relation to the federal government.

The federal government has certain *express powers* (also called *enumerated powers*), which are powers spelled out in the Constitution, including the right to levy taxes, declare war, and regulate interstate and foreign commerce.

Also, the *Necessary and Proper Clause* gives the federal government the *implied power* to pass any law "necessary and proper" to execute its express powers.

Enumerated powers of the Federal Government are contained in Article I, Section 8 of the U.S. Constitution.

Other powers—the *reserved powers*—are reserved to the people or the states under the 10th Amendment. The Supreme Court decision significantly expanded the power delegated to the federal government in *McCulloch v. Maryland* (1819) and the 13th, 14th and 15th, Amendments to the Constitution following the **Civil War**.

Interpretation of the Constitution

Mode of Constitutional interpretation

There is disagreement over the analytical construct for interpreting the Constitution.

Living Constitution (closely aligned with Realism and Realist judges) changes to meet the needs of society.

Mode 1: *legislative history* considers the intent during the enactment.

Mode 2: *interpreting the text* has increased enormously as a mode of analysis.

Scalia: what I look for in the Constitution is what I look for in a statute: the *original meaning of the text*, not what the original draftsmen intended.

Ideological groupings

Ideology is a system of fundamental beliefs that specify appropriate and inappropriate conduct.

Judicial decisions often derive or, at least, align with the political ideology of judges, as has been empirically shown.

Conservatives on the court espouse a limited role for government in the private affairs of citizens, let markets rule.

Liberals on the court espouse an expanded role for the government in the private affairs of citizens.

Legal criticisms

Natural law is the unwritten body of universal moral principles underlying the ethical and legal norms by which human conduct is evaluated and governed.

Textualism is where judges have no authority to pursue broader social purposes or write new laws.

Strict constructionism was described by the late Justice Scalia as a degraded form of textualism.

Legislative intent looks for objectified intent as a reasonable person would gather from the text of the law placed alongside the remainder of the corpus juris;

the primary object of interpreting statutes is to ascertain the legislative intent *or* the meaning which the subject is authorized to understand the legislature intended; it is undemocratic to have the meaning of a law determined by what the lawgiver means rather than what the lawgiver promulgated. The intent of the lawgiver, not the judges.

Originalism (or *original intent*): what was meant by the drafters at the time it was written. Original meaning proposes what a reasonable person living when the language was ratified would believe the meaning.

Legal realism permits modification if furthering the function intended.

Living constitutionalism proposes that the Constitution must change.

Critical legal studies focus on race, gender, sex, weight, Marxism, and conflict.

The 4th and 5th Amendments Protections for Criminal Defendants

The Fourth Amendment to the U.S. Constitution protects persons and corporations from overzealous investigative activities by the government. It protects the rights of the people from unreasonable search and seizure by the government and permits people to be secure in their persons, houses, papers, and effects.

Reasonable searches are those (in most instances) predicated on a search warrant based on probable cause. Search warrants specifically state the *place and scope* of the authorized search. General searches beyond the specified area are forbidden.

Warrantless searches generally are permitted only 1) incident to arrest, 2) where evidence is in "plain view," or 3) where evidence likely will be destroyed. Evidence obtained from an unreasonable search and seizure is considered tainted and, under the exclusionary rule, is generally excluded from criminal prosecutions.

The Fifth Amendment provides that no person "shall be compelled in any criminal case to be a witness against himself." A person cannot be compelled to give testimony against himself or herself, although nontestimonial evidence, such as fingerprints and body fluids, may be required. This protection applies only to natural persons, not corporations and partnerships.

Based on Supreme Court decisions, it is improper for a jury to infer guilt from the defendant's exercise of their constitutional right to remain silent.

However, if the government wants to obtain evidence from one who has taken the Fifth, it can offer the person immunity, which means the government would agree not to prosecute the person based on the testimony they would give. The Fifth Amendment protects against double jeopardy, whereby a criminal defendant may not be tried twice for the same crime.

If the same criminal act involves several crimes, the accused may be tried for each crime without violating the double jeopardy clause. If the same act violates the laws of other jurisdictions, each jurisdiction may charge and try the accused.

Comprehensive Glossary of Legal Terms

Over 2,100 essential legal terms defined and explained. An excellent reference source for law students, practitioners, and readers seeking an understanding of legal vocabulary and its application.

Landmark U.S. Supreme Court Cases: Essential Summaries

Learn important constitutional cases that shaped American law. Understand how the evolving needs of society intersect with the U.S. Constitution. Summaries of seminal Supreme Court cases focused on legal issues, underlying principles, and judicial decisions.

Visit our Amazon store

Everything You Always Wanted to Know About...

Chemistry	American History
Physics	American Law
Cell and Molecular Biology	American Government and Politics
Organismal Biology	Comparative Government and Politics
Psychology	World History
Environmental Science	European History
Human Geography	

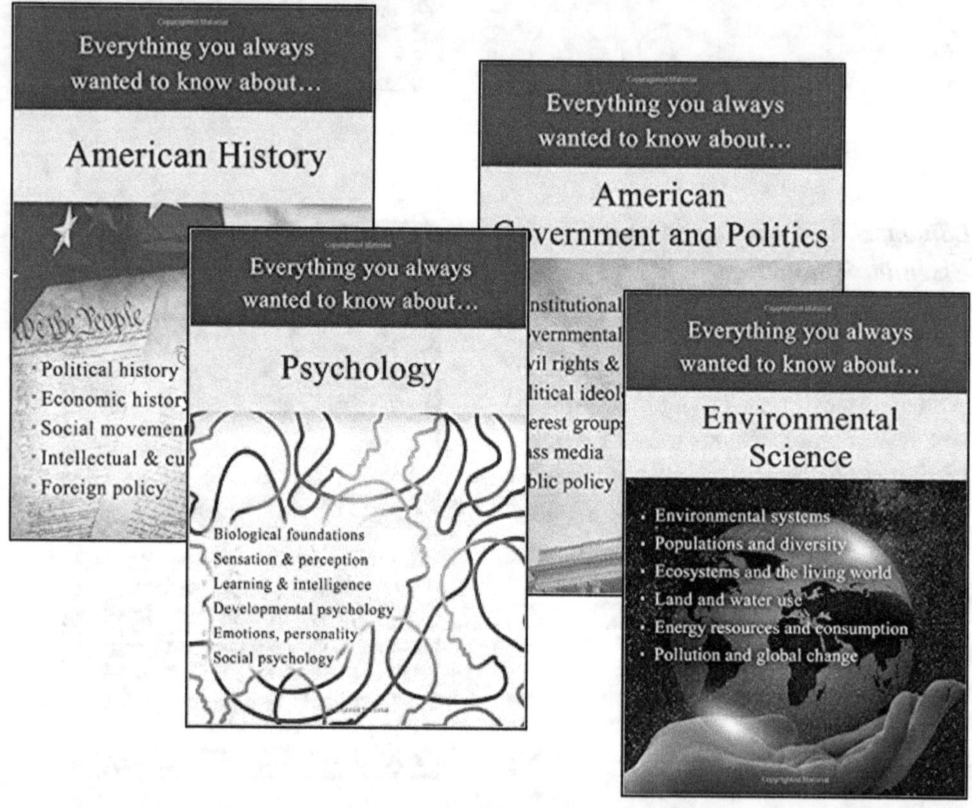

Visit our Amazon store